INSIDE
TriSpectives
Technical®

Elliot Sanders and Janalyn Sanders

INSIDE TriSpectives Technical®

By Elliot Sanders and Janalyn Sanders

Published by:
OnWord Press
2530 Camino Entrada
Santa Fe, NM 87505-4835 USA

First Edition, 1997

SAN 694-0269

10 9 8 7 6 5 4 3 2 1

Printed in the United States of America

Library of Congress Cataloging-in-Publication Data

Sanders, Elliot, 1963-
    Inside 3D/EYE TriSpectives Technical / Elliot Sanders and Janalyn Sanders. -- 1st ed.
        p.   cm.
    Includes index.
    ISBN 1-56690-108-1
    1. Computer graphics. 2. TriSpectives. 3. Three-dimensional display systems. 4. Computer-aided design.   I. Sanders, Janalyn, 1962-   . II. Title.

T385.S2495   1997
006.6'93--dc21   97-4046
                                                                                    CIP

Trademarks

TriSpectives Technical and TriSpectives are registered trademarks of 3D/Eye, a division of Visionary Design Systems, Inc. TriWizard is a trademark of 3D/Eye. OnWord Press is a registered trademark of High Mountain Press, Inc. All other terms mentioned in this book that are known to be trademarks or service marks have been appropriately capitalized. OnWord Press cannot attest to the accuracy of this information. Use of a term in this book should not be regarded as affecting the validity of any trademark or service mark.

Warning and Disclaimer

This book is designed to provide information on the usage of the TriSpectives Technical software. Every effort has been made to make the book as complete, accurate, and up to date as possible; however, no warranty or fitness is implied.

The information is provided on an "as is" basis. The authors and OnWord Press shall have neither liability nor responsibility to any person or entity with respect to any loss or damages in connection with or arising from the information contained in this book.

About the Authors

Elliot Sanders received a B.S. in biological sciences from the University of California-Irvine, and an M.S. in biomedical engineering from the University of Virginia. He currently works as a research engineer designing medical devices.

Janalyn Sanders has a B.S. in biological sciences from the University of California-Irvine. She has worked as a marine biologist and technical writer and editor for several years.

Elliot and Janalyn both enjoy sailing, kayaking, and camping. Several chapters of this book were written in a campground north of San Francisco, CA.

Acknowledgments

We would like to thank God. We would also like to thank the folks at High Mountain Press, especially Barbara Kohl and Heidi Schulman for their patience, persistence, and chutzpah. We are also grateful to the crew at 3D/EYE for their assistance.

Special thanks to the technical reviewers of the manuscript, especially Shaun Murphy, technical marketing manager at 3D/EYE, and Jason Key, technical marketing representative at 3D/EYE.

Elliot Sanders and Janalyn Sanders

OnWord Press...

Dan Raker, President
Dale Bennie, Information Publishing Group Director
David Talbott, Acquisitions and Development Director
Carol Leyba, Associate Publisher
Barbara Kohl, Acquisitions Editor
Heidi Schulman, Project Editor
Daril Bentley, Project Editor
Jean Cooksey, Project Editor
Cynthia Welch, Production Manager
Liz Bennie, Marketing Manager
Lauri Hogan, Marketing Services Manager
Kristie Reilly, Assistant Editor
Lynne Egensteiner, Cover designer, Illustrator

Contents

Chapter 7
Arranging Models in Virtual Space   103

Chapter 8
Enhancing Scenes   115

Chapter 9
Lighting and Shadow   131

Chapter 10
Using 3D Text   149

Chapter 11
Creating Animations 159

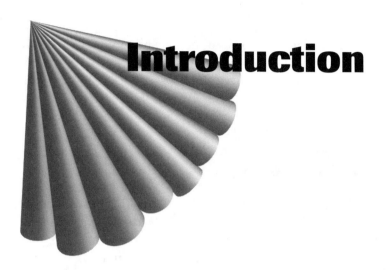

Introduction

Computer-aided design and 3D modeling have reached the stage of critical mass. With applications covering an enormous range from parts design in manufacturing, to architectural uses, animation, and the arts, experienced and beginning 3D modelers alike are turning to computers to solve problems and create opportunities that once were possible only in the world of imagination.

TriSpectives is especially notable in the arena of 3D design because it combines simplicity of use with capabilities often found only in extremely advanced systems. The goal of this book is to help the experienced and novice alike to rely on TriSpectives Technical as an effective and enjoyable tool for navigating the realm of 3D design. The text is simple in order to avoid confusion among new users. However, advanced concepts are also discussed.

The first half of this book is a basic introductory guide to the way in which TriSpectives handles the concept of 3D modeling; the second is more technically detailed. Even if you have extensive experience in 3D modeling, we urge you to read and work through the entire book. TriSpectives has its own ways of handling 3D modeling issues and they may vary from the CAD programs which with you are familiar.

This book is designed to explore the capabilities of TriSpectives Technical, but many of its exercises work equally well for the non-technical version of TriSpectives and TriWizard. Whatever product you may be using, we believe that *INSIDE TriSpectives Technical* will arm you with practical, accessible information to ensure that you use this dynamic 3D modeling tool to its best advantage.

Book Structure

Chapters 1 and 2 introduce the TriSpectives Technical interface, retrieval of parts from a catalog, and the design of simple 2D and 3D objects. Chapters 3 and 4 illustrate the creation of more complex models and worlds. Chapter 5 is focused on altering the surface appearance of models, and Chapter 6, the creation of technical documents with TriSpectives models. Chapter 7 demonstrates how to arrange models, and thereby provides information on the distinct advantages of TriSpectives Technical over other 3D modeling systems.

Chapters 8 and 9 introduce the subjects of rendering, and the process of adding surface effects, lighting, and cameras. Subsequent chapters discuss the creation and arranging of 3D text, and the creation and editing of 3D animations.

Typographical Conventions

The names of TriSpectives Technical functionality interface items are capitalized. Examples include menus, menu options, toolbar names, tool buttons, and dialog box options. Samples appear below.

Open the text editor and select Insert | Object.

To create multiple views, right-click in a scene and choose either Horizontal Split or Vertical Split from the pop-up menu.

Because you want the image to fit the surface, set Image Project to Natural. Click on Apply.

User input is italicized. Examples are names for files, file extensions, directories, dimension settings, and so on.

Double-click on the *Specs.doc* file, then click on OK.

Navigate the *Inside* directory on the companion CD.

Enter a value of *.25* and click on OK.

The resulting models will either be native to the application to which they are being exported (*.3ds*, *.dxf*, *.obj*, *.wrl*), or become facet models (*.raw*, *.stl*).

Italics are also used to indicate emphasis.

General function and single keyboard keys appear enclosed in angle brackets.

<Enter>

<Shift>

Key sequences—instructions to hold a key down while clicking the mouse or pressing another key—are linked with a plus sign.

<Ctrl>+click

<Ctrl>+<S>

⇨ **TIP:** *Tips on functionality usage, shortcuts, and other information aimed at saving you time and toil appear like this.*

✓ **NOTE:** *Information on features and tasks that is not immediately obvious or intuitive appears in notes.*

Companion CD-ROM

The companion CD contains a time-out version of TriSpectives Technical and files used in the exercises throughout the book. The exercise files are located in the *Inside* directory (level), while the program files are located in the root directory and several directories enumerated below. If you have already purchased and loaded TriSpectives Technical, skip the next section.

TriSpectives Technical Demo Files

If you already have TriSpectives Technical 2.0 on your system, do not install the software on the CD. If you have already installed TriSpectives Professional 1.0 on your system, you need not uninstall the older software to load the software on the CD. TriSpectives Professional 1.0 and TriSpectives Technical 2.0 can run simultaneously.

To install TriSpectives Technical from the Windows Explorer or File Manager, double-click on *SETUP.EXE* in the root directory of the CD-ROM and follow the setup instructions. Windows 95 users may also choose to use the Add/Remove Programs Control Panel or the Install TriSpectives Technical option during Autoplay.

Several screens into the setup procedure, you will be prompted for your name, company, and serial number. You can leave the first two fields blank, but you must input something in the serial number field. To satisfy this requirement, type the word "book" in the field, and click on Next.

You will be prompted to select one of the three loading options summarized below.

- Typical—Load all software and translators (about 135 Mb).

- Compact—Loads minimal set of options in addition to software and translators (175 Mb).

- Custom—You can choose the options to load to the hard disk.

After selecting the desired loading option, the software will complete the installation. Several minutes are required to complete the loading, depending on the selected option and your computer hardware. When you load the software for the first time, you will see a dialog that requests a code word. If you do not have a code word, you are prompted to hit the Evaluate key, which initiates the 30-day evaluation period.

During the evaluation period, you have the option to purchase the software from 3D/EYE. Upon purchasing the software, you are supplied with a new serial number and a code word which activates a perpetual license, and a complete set of manuals.

TriSpectives Technical program files on the CD are divided into the directories described below.

File name	Size (bytes)	File name
BROCHURE	7,036,2453	3D/EYE product information.
CATALOGS	11,867,136	Various catalogs used to create scenes in TriSpectives Technical.
IMAGES	87,582,148	All TriSpectives textures.
MANUALS	22,138,823	TriSpectives Technical online help files.
MMDEMO	58,552,438	Interactive multimedia demo of TriSpectives Technical. A sound card is strongly recommended to get the most information from the demo.
MS_VFW	1,427,692	This directory contains the Microsoft Video Viewer used by the TriSpectives Technical multimedia demo.
SUPPORT	65,848	SUPPORT.TXT contains information on contacting 3D/EYE Technical Support.
TEMPLATE	568,832	TriSpectives templates used when creating a new TriSpectives Technical scene.

For documentation errata, technical notes, and other up-to-date news concerning 3D/EYE products, see the company's web site, *www.eye.com.*

Inside Files

Consider copying the files in the *Inside* directory to your hard disk. If you choose to copy the files instead of accessing them from the CD, use the File Manager or DOS commands to copy them to a new subdirectory on your hard disk. The subdirectory would contain both the files copied from the CD as well as any files you create in the course of performing the exercises in the book. The following table lists the files in the *Inside* directory by name and size in bytes.

File name	Size (bytes)	File name	Size (bytes)
Piston.tmd	485,376	Pistons.avi	557,568
Blimp.3ds	29,096	Complex.tif	106,188
Complex.tmd	239,616	Ace.tif	1,356
gsilver.ti	2,638	jack.tif	2,662
Seven.tif	1,602	Specs.doc	5,120
Two.tif	1,422	Drive.tmd	680,960
Explode.tmd	845,312	House.tmd	4,001,792
INSIDE.tsc	679,936	Magic.tmd	1,865,216
Magic_show.tmd	1,863,680	Office.tmd	1,853,440
Picnic.tmd	2,421,248	Room.tmd	4,001,792
Training.tmd	859,136	Truck.tmd	795,136

1

Introduction to TriSpectives

The traditional process of guiding an idea from initial conception through prototype to market is complex, involving many people and software programs. The development process may have involved creating black and white overheads to pitch the idea, employing an engineer skilled in computer-aided drafting (CAD) to turn the two-dimensional (2D) sketch into a three-dimensional (3D) design, hiring a draftsperson to create detailed manual or computer drawings, and working with a designer and yet another software package to create product brochures and manuals.

TriSpectives simplifies the traditional process, reducing the number of software programs and people needed to develop a project. It is a single program that performs 3D modeling, rendering, texture mapping, and animation functions in a user-friendly environment. Presentations are also enhanced by TriSpectives' functionality: objects can be rendered with enough precision to satisfy an engineer, yet with enough visual appeal for an artist or architect. TriSpectives can also reduce a project's production time because collaborators can copy your preliminary 3D model and begin their work before the model is complete. Perhaps most importantly, you can create directly in 3D.

From concept to prototype to marketing using TriSpectives.

After working in a 2D world, designing in a 3D TriSpectives world often requires a few initial adjustments. The following section highlights four areas that present differences when moving from 2D to 3D.

Navigation

To understand navigating in a virtual world, imagine you are looking through a camera. To move from side to side or up and down, pan through a scene. To get closer or farther away, zoom in or out. To view the scene from a new angle, both you and the camera orbit the scene.

Assigning Values

Many CAD programs employ the values x, y, and z when creating and positioning models. TriSpectives eliminates this engineering oriented approach and instead uses the terms length, width and height.

Moving and Locating Objects

Locating Objects Within a Scene

There are three methods of locating objects in the 3D world: (1) approximately, by dragging with a mouse; (2) precisely, by using a property sheet in a dialog box; and (3) by using the TriBall tool, which can locate both exactly and approximately. Each of these methods will be described in subsequent chapters.

> ✓ **NOTE:** *The term "object" may be used to refer to a variety of items such as shapes, models, lights, and cameras. See Chapter 2 for a discussion of shapes, models, and objects.*

The TriBall tool is effective in locating objects.

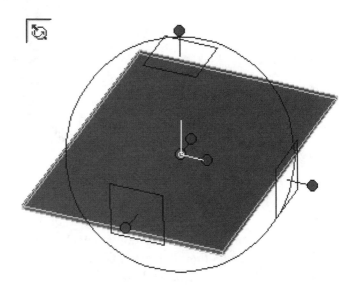

Drag and Drop

Drag and drop is an effective way of using the more than 1,500 predefined shapes, colors, textures, and models TriSpectives provides. (A detailed discussion of these objects and their properties appears in Chapter 2.) Use this method to add shapes or models to a scene, apply color or texture to surfaces, and insert features such as holes or slots into objects.

Shape and Object Behavior

In TriSpectives, shapes have intelligence; they contain data such as size, position, appearance (color, texture, bumps), cross-section geometry, and surface reshaping. These shapes, called IntelliShapes, are discussed in Chapter 2.

IntelliShapes comprised of cross-section geometry.

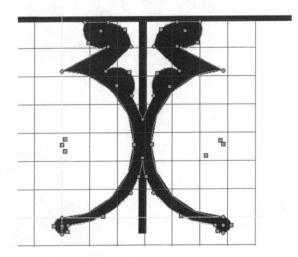

Models consist of one or more shapes. Even when several shapes are used to create a model, each shape can be edited on its own. Models not only contain intelligence, they relate intelligently to each other. For example, when a chair is placed on a floor it naturally orients itself upright; a lamp does the same when dropped onto a desktop. When adding colors and textures to an object, TriSpectives determines the most logical application. Of course, the application can be altered to suit specific needs.

These models were dragged and dropped onto the scene from a catalog.

You can also control how models' dimensions relate to each other. For example, the length of a model can be designated as twice that of the width.

A Tour of TriSpectives

Start TriSpectives with a new blank scene. Look at the TriSpectives window illustrated below. The window you open may look a bit different because toolbars and catalog browsers are movable, allowing customized environments.

**Embedded
Toolbars**

**Menu
Bar**

**Catalog
Browser**

Workview

**Status
Bar**

**Floating
Toolbar**

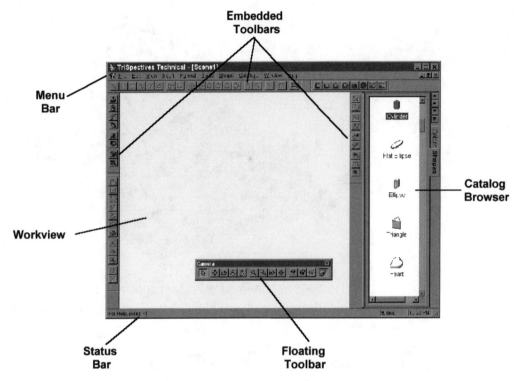

Anatomy of the TriSpectives window.

Menus

Start the tour by locating the TriSpectives program logo next to the words *TriSpectives Technical [Scene1]* in the upper left of the screen. Click on the logo. A drop-down menu of program window-related functions appears, including an option to close the program. Note the menu bar just below the TriSpectives logo, which displays 10 menu headings. If the current scene is maximized within the program window, the TriSpectives scene icon will also be visible. Menu bar functions relate to the scene file that is currently active.

Click on the Scene logo icon. The menu that drops down from the scene logo icon resembles the program window drop-down menu. However, there are a few exceptions. First, menu functions adjust the scene window, rather than the program window. Second, the hot key for Close is now <Ctrl>+F4 rather than <Alt>+F4. Third, an additional menu command, Next, activates the next open scene. Take a few minutes to examine the other drop-down menus in the menu bar by clicking on a menu heading and moving the mouse over adjacent headings to view other menus.

> ➡ **TIP:** *Multiple windows (each with their own scenes) can remain open simultaneously. If you are working with more than one scene at a time, drop-down menu options apply only to the scene currently selected. To perform menu functions on another scene, click on the top of the desired scene window or use the Next command to flip through open scenes.*

Toolbars

TriSpectives' 13 toolbars access most tools. Toolbars can be added to the screen by turning them on, or hidden by turning them off. You can display multiple toolbars, but doing so will reduce the screen space available for scenes and models.

To explore toolbar options, select View | Toolbars. You can select or deselect a toolbar with a click of the mouse. Select the 3D Shapes and Camera toolbars, and click on OK.

*Turn toolbars on and off by
selecting or deselecting.*

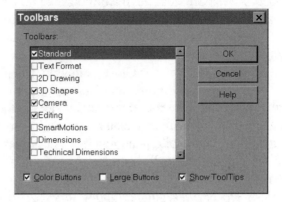

Toolbars can be moved around within a scene, allowing greater flexibility when viewing your work. They can be relocated or embedded in the top, bottom, left, or right of the workview window using the drag and drop method. They can also be dragged on top of the workview and used as floating toolbars.

> ✓ **NOTE:** *Embedded toolbars change the size of the workview by automatically stacking to avoid overlapping each other. Floating toolbars are allowed to overlap, but will not alter the size of the workview.*

Toolbars are also location sensitive; they will change shape and orientation when dragged to new locations. Click on a toolbar and drag it from the top of the window to the left side, and note the effect.

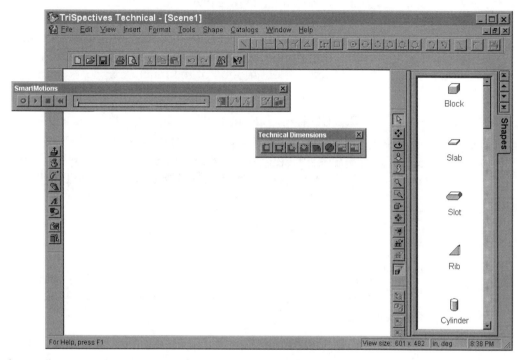

Any toolbar can be moved by dragging it to a new location.

Status Bar

When you first started TriSpectives, the status bar should have appeared automatically in the lower left of the window. The status bar provides valuable input about the function that a menu selection or toolbar button is about to perform. To explore the status bar, complete the following steps.

1. In the menu bar, select View. If there is a check mark on the Status Bar line, the status bar is on. If the check mark is absent, click on the Status Bar line to turn the status bar on.

2. Position the mouse over one of the toolbars, but do not click on a toolbar button. As you pause over a button, a floating title appears on the screen, providing a brief description of the button's function. Note that a more detailed description of the function appears in the status bar.

3. Click on File in the menu bar. When the pull-down menu appears, position the mouse over one of the menu options. Note the expanded description in the status bar. Move the mouse over other menu choices and note the expanded descriptions in the status bar.

Catalog Browser

The Catalog Browser lets you store and retrieve hundreds of models, textures, animations, colors, and other features. One advantage of the Browser is that it saves time by eliminating the need for file opener utilities.

Like the status bar and toolbars, the Catalog Browser can be turned on and off from the View menu and repositioned on the screen. It can also be resized; to do so, grab its inner edge and drag it toward or away from the middle of the scene. The Browser's tab and scroll button features are especially helpful when working with several open catalogs.

Items contained in catalogs are represented by thumbnail icons; these icons can be given descriptive names for easier identification. You can work with available TriSpectives catalogs, or create custom catalogs to suit your needs. Catalogs are shared by projects and can be opened and closed under the Catalog menu. (Creating groups of catalogs for different types of projects will be covered in detail in Chapter 2.)

Thumbnail views of objects can be browsed in catalogs.

To create a new catalog for a specific project, complete the following exercise.

1. Verify that the Catalog Browser is open. If it is not, select View | Catalog Browser from the menu bar.

2. Select the Catalogs | New menu option to create a new catalog. The catalog appears in the Catalog Browser, and catalogs that were open earlier seem to have disappeared. However, if you click on the up arrow at the right side of the Catalog Browser, you will see they are still open. Return to the new catalog.

3. Rename the new catalog by choosing Catalogs | Save As. The choice of where to place the new catalog is completely up to you. Choose an appropriate place and name your catalog by typing *My Catalog* into the File name field.

Saving a new catalog.

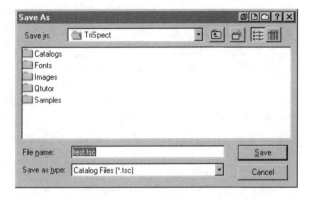

✓ **NOTE:** *Catalog files must have a file extension of .tsc to be recognized as catalogs by TriSpectives. However, when you save a catalog you need only type the name; TriSpectives automatically gives it the .tsc extension.*

4. Click on Save or press <Enter>. The catalog's new name will appear on the catalog tab in place of the old one.

5. Put the catalog away by choosing Catalogs | Close. You will be accessing it later.

You are now ready to create a TriSpectives model.

Design Session

Your first objective is to create a rough concept of a table. Each step or series of steps that follows illustrates an important part of the TriSpectives design process. This simple project demonstrates the ease and power of TriSpectives; you will work on more complicated projects as you move through the book. For now, follow the steps in each category.

Begin the Process

1. Open a new scene by selecting File | New from the menu bar. Accept Blank Scene as the format by clicking on OK.

2. Select Format | Units, and choose inches for length units. Click on OK.

3. Select View | Toolbars from the menu bar. Click on the boxes next to Camera and 3D Shapes, and then click on OK.

4. For the moment, close all catalogs by selecting Catalogs | Close All from the menu bar.

5. Select Catalogs | Catalog Sets and choose the Default catalog set. Click on Open, and then click on Done in the dialog box.

6. Use the arrow buttons to scroll through the catalogs until you see the Shapes catalog. Then click on the Shapes catalog to bring it to the top.

Drag and Drop a Shape

1. Click on the Block catalog object and drag it into the scene. Drop it by releasing the mouse button.

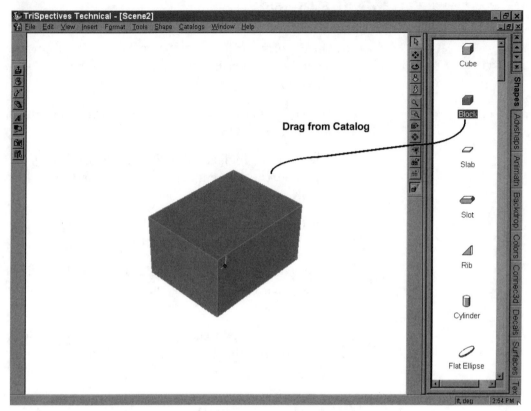

Drag and drop the block shape into the scene.

Modify the Shape

Edit IntelliShapes button.

1. Ensure that the Edit IntelliShapes button on the 3D Shapes toolbar is depressed. Click on the block. The small ball-shaped objects protruding from the block are called "Sizebox handles" and serve as grips.

2. To change the shape of the object, position the mouse over the rightmost ball. When the cursor changes from an arrow to a hand, click and drag the grip an inch or

two. Once again, position the mouse over the right ball. Click on the right mouse button. When the Edit Sizebox button appears, click on it.

Using the right mouse button, click on an IntelliShape handle (grip) to access the Edit Sizebox button.

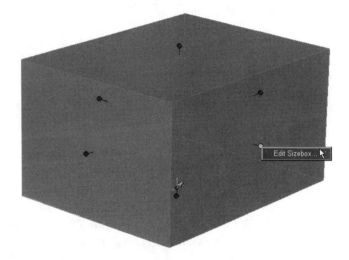

Edit Sizebox...

3. Enter a Length of *3*, a Width of *3,* and a Height of *30* in the appropriate fields, and then press <Enter> or click on OK. The shape you have created will be the post for the table.

Change the Point of View

1. Select the Orbit Camera button from the Camera toolbar. Note that the mouse pointer changes shape when you move it over the scene.

2. Rotate the scene by holding down the left mouse button and dragging the scene. Turn the scene until you are viewing the bottom portion of the block. Deselect the Orbit Camera.

✓ **NOTE:** *Orbiting around a scene changes your view of an object by moving the camera, not by moving the object.*

Camera toolbar with Orbit
Camera tool highlighted.

3. Click on a blank space in the scene to deselect the block.

Add Another Shape

1. Click on the Slab catalog object and drag it to the center of the bottom of the block you created. When you are on center, a green dot will appear. This dot is known as a landmark.

✓ **NOTE:** *TriSpectives is a feature-based modeling system; each of the shapes in a model remains editable on its own.*

2. Drop the slab onto the bottom of the block by releasing the mouse button.

A green landmark appears on the
center of the block surface.

Fit Scene button.

3. The slab probably fills most of the scene. To adjust the image in the scene, use the Fit Scene button on the Camera toolbar.

SmartSnap is a powerful positioning tool that can be used to align shapes using center points, middle points, edges, corners, and other key positions. As a shape is dragged over the surface of another shape, green dots (landmarks) will appear indicating centers and corners, and green lines will indicate edges or surfaces. SmartSnap features automatically appear when a new shape is dragged in from a catalog onto a surface, but they must be activated by depressing the <Shift> key when repositioning shapes already in the scene. To use the SmartSnap feature with shapes in the scene, verify that the anchor of the shape is set to "Slide along the surfaces."

Resize the Slab

1. Position the mouse pointer over the slab, carefully avoiding the size handles, and click on the object with the right mouse button.

2. Select IntelliShape Properties from the pop-up menu.

3. Click on the Sizebox tab at the top of the IntelliShape Properties dialog box. (The IntelliShape Properties dialog box will be discussed further in Chapter 2.)

4. Enter the values shown in the following illustration for Length, Width, and Height. Click on OK or press <Enter>.

IntelliShape Properties dialog.

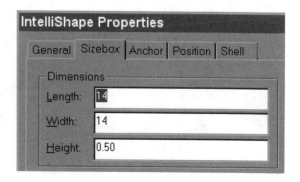

5. Add another slab to the bottom center of the previous slab. Edit the size using the Sizebox tab in the IntelliShape Properties dialog box. Give this new slab dimensions of 15, 15, and 0.5 inches.

Add Another Block

1. Use the Orbit Camera tool to reposition the scene. When you have a view of the top of the block, turn the Orbit Camera tool off.

2. Drag a new block out of the catalog. Drop it on the center top surface of the table post.

Intermediate step in the table model.

3. Turn Edit IntelliShapes off by deselecting the button.

✓ **NOTE:** *Be patient if your objects try to cling to each other. This clinging reflects the fact that shapes, by default behavior, are instructed to relate to other shapes they contact.*

Modify the New Block

1. To enter model edit mode, verify that the Edit IntelliShapes and the Edit Surfaces and Edges buttons are not depressed. Then click once on the model. The model's outline color will change depending on which function is activated.

- A *blue* outline means that you will be editing the properties of the whole model, whether it is comprised of one shape or many.
- A *yellow* outline means only the highlighted IntelliShape will be affected by any change.
- A *green* outline means that only the single highlighted surface will be altered.

3D Shapes toolbar.

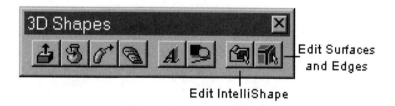

2. Click on the new block until the yellow outline appears, indicating that only the IntelliShape is selected.

3. Click on the block with the right mouse button, and then select IntelliShape Properties from the pop-up menu.

4. Select the Sizebox tab and enter the values of *23* for Length, *23* for Width, and *0.5* for Height. Click on OK or press <Enter>.

✓ **NOTE:** *You have created a slab from a block shape. Except for respective initial dimensions, the properties of these two IntelliShapes are virtually identical.*

5. Turn Edit IntelliShapes back on. If you do not click on the Edit IntelliShapes button, your next feature will be an independent model.

✓ **NOTE:** *When selection tools are off, new shapes are added to the scene as independent models. This becomes important when working with more complex modeling tools in Chapters 3 and 4.*

6. To complete the table, add either another slab or block to the center of the previous one, and then edit the dimensions using the IntelliShapes Properties dialog box. Set the dimensions for the final shape to 22, 22, and 0.5 inches.

When you drop the new slab onto the existing block it becomes the same color as the rest of the model, confirming that the block is part of the model.

Change the Model Color

1. Scroll through the catalogs until you find the Colors Catalog tab. Click on it to bring the tab to the top.

2. Choose a color that pleases you. Click and drag it to the top block of the model. The first model is now complete.

✓ **NOTE:** *Dragging a color onto a model will affect the entire model unless the Edit Surfaces and Edges button is depressed.*

3. Save your work by selecting File | Save As. Enter the file name *Table*. Click on Save. Using the Orbit Camera tool, view the model from several different angles.

Completed table model.

Place a Model in a Catalog

1. To save the model for use in another scene, first save it to a catalog by selecting Catalogs | Open. Find the catalog titled *My Catalog* created earlier in this chapter.

2. Verify that the Edit IntelliShapes button is not selected and that no shapes are highlighted in the scene.

3. Click on the model and drag it to *My Catalog.* Drop the model in the catalog by releasing the mouse button. A plus sign appears at the bottom of the pointer when you have successfully dragged the model into the catalog.

4. A thumbnail version of the model should appear in the catalog. Its title is *UnNamed.* Rename the file by clicking in the title field and typing *Concept.*

➥ **TIP:** *Take some time to examine the TriSpectives catalogs and locate those which interest you. As described in Chapter 2, you can also create your own set of catalogs as the default.*

2 Designing with TriSpectives

This chapter builds on a basic understanding of TriSpectives design by taking a closer look at design tools and methods. Topics include the use of 2D shapes, facet models, and (3D) IntelliShapes to create models; discussion of shape, model, and style properties; and the use of catalogs in organization. The design session is focused on enhancing design initiated in Chapter 1.

The Concept of Shape

In the two-dimensional world, the concept of shape often means the outer form or line of an object. In TriSpectives design, a shape is a self-contained unit that serves as a building block for a model. Three items are available to help build designs: IntelliShapes (3D), facet models, and 2D shapes.

2D Shapes

2D shapes can be added to a scene to give texture and the ability to cast and accept shadows. Follow the steps in the exercise below to create a 2D shape, in this case a figure eight.

Insert 2D Shape button.

Look At button.

Circle Radius button.

Circle Diameter button.

1. Select Insert | 2D Shape from the menu bar, or click on the Insert 2D Shape button on the 3D Shapes toolbar. The cursor will change to a pointer with shapes attached to it. Click on a blank area of the scene.

2. The drawing grid that appears will probably not be flat from your point of view. If you would like to look straight at the grid, select the Look At button on the Camera toolbar and click anywhere on the grid.

3. Turn on the 2D Technical Editing toolbar by clicking in the toolbar area above the scene with the right mouse button. Select the 2D Technical Editing option. The 2D Technical Drawing toolbar will automatically be activated when you select to insert a 2D shape.

4. Draw a circle by selecting the Circle Radius button from the 2D Technical Drawing toolbar. Click in two places on the drawing grid; the distance between clicks will define the circle's radius. Use the Circle Diameter tool to create a circle that intersects the first one.

Draw two intersecting circles using the tools on the 2D Technical Drawing toolbar.

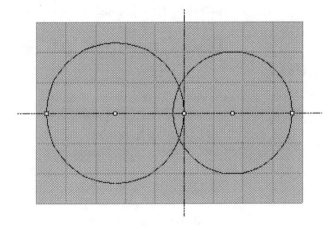

*Trim Curve
Between Curves
button.*

5. Click on the Trim Curve Between Curves button on the 2D Technical Editing toolbar. The status bar will display a message asking you to specify which curve to cut. Pick one of the interior portions of the circles. A green asterisk will appear on the curve.

6. TriSpectives will now ask that you "specify the first curve to cut with." Select the other circle, and then the first circle again. TriSpectives will trim away the part you selected in step 5.

7. Repeat the trim process to remove the inner portion of the other circle, and then deselect the Trim button. The result will be the outline of a figure eight.

*Trim operation completed
using the Trim Curve
Between Curve tool.*

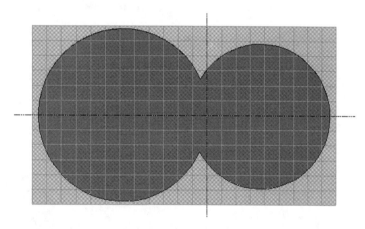

8. Select the two portions of the outlines by holding down the <Shift> key and clicking on each portion.

*Offset 2D Curves
button.*

9. Click the Offset 2D Curves button on the 2D Technical Editing toolbar. In the pop-up dialog box, type in a value of *10* for the distance and click on Apply. Experiment with different values and the Flip Direction toggle, clicking on Apply every time you want to update the changes.

10. When you have created a figure eight design similar to the one in the following illustration, select OK.

Lines duplicated with the Offset 2D Curves tool, creating a figure eight.

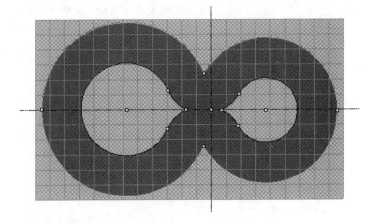

11. Click on Finish Shape. The 2D shape is automatically shaded. Use the Orbit Camera tool to view all sides of the new geometry.

Orbit Camera button.

Finished shaded figure eight.

✓ **NOTE**: *2D design tools can also be used in 3D cross section design, as discussed throughout this book. However, 2D shapes cannot be turned into 3D shapes.*

Facet Models

Facet models are comprised of hundreds, sometimes thousands, of smaller surfaces called "facets." You can import models from a variety of other formats and translate them into facet models. (Non-facet models can also be imported and used in their original forms.)

✓ **NOTE**: *When working with facet models, you can edit for scale factors (length, width, and height) and appearance (color, textures, and decals). However, the underlying geometry of facet models cannot be edited.*

The following exercise involves importing a 3D Studio model of a blimp from the *Inside* directory on the companion CD.

1. Use the right mouse button to click on a blank area in the scene and select Rendering from the pop-up menu. Select Style | Facet Shading as the style of rendering. This option offers an accurate representation of the model to be inserted. Click on OK.

2. Ensure that the Edit IntelliShapes and Edit Surfaces and Edges buttons are not depressed. Select Insert | Model from the menu bar.

Edit IntelliShapes button.

Edit Surfaces and Edge button.

Fit Scene button.

3. Browse the *Inside* directory on the CD to locate the *Blimp.3ds* file. Click on Open. Use the Fit Scene tool on the Camera toolbar to bring the Blimp model into full view.

3D Studio model of a blimp.

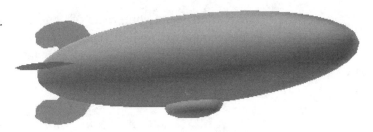

Window Zoom button.

4. Use the Window Zoom command to zoom in on the nose section of the blimp. Rotate the model to view the many facets used to produce this curved surface.

✓ **NOTE:** *To gain a better understanding of facet models, set the scene rendering to Wireframe mode. Note that even flat surfaces, such as the tail fins of the blimp model, are represented by a large number of triangular facets.*

5. Select the Edit IntelliShapes button and click on the model with the right mouse button. Select Facet Model Properties at the bottom of the pop-up menu. Take a few minutes to familiarize yourself with the options. Additional discussion of object properties appears later in this chapter.

Even when you drag and drop an IntelliShape model from a TriSpectives catalog into a scene, it is initially placed as a facet model to conserve memory. However, unlike an imported facet model, you can return later and edit the geometry used to create the facet model. This process is explained further in the following section.

IntelliShapes

IntelliShapes, which are always 3D models, are an important design tool. As mentioned in Chapter 1, IntelliShapes are the building blocks for your models. A small database of information is maintained for each IntelliShape you use or create. Each database contains the following information about the shape:

- size
- anchor location and behavior
- position
- shell and bevel properties
- interaction with other objects
- model creation geometry

IntelliShapes are stored in catalogs and can be dragged and dropped in a scene. Insert a pencil shape in the scene by taking the following steps.

1. Verify that the Catalog Browser is selected from the View menu. Then select Catalogs | Open from the menu bar.

2. Navigate to the directory in which TriSpectives is installed. Open the *Catalogs* directory.

3. Double-click on the *Showcase.tsc* file. Take a minute to examine the Showcase catalog, and then drag and drop the pencil model into the scene. Be careful not to drop the new object onto any existing objects.

Pencil model in the
Showcase catalog.

When the model is first dropped, it is represented by a facet model and its Sizebox is active.

➡ **TIP:** *For time-saving yet dynamic screen resolution, set rendering to Smooth Shading and check the Show Textures option. The Rendering dialog box can be accessed by clicking on a blank part of the scene with the right mouse button.*

Although the initial model is a facet model, the pencil model is essentially composed of four IntelliShapes. To enhance editing possibilities, regenerate the facet model as an IntelliShape model according to the steps below.

1. Verify that the Edit IntelliShapes button is depressed. Click on the eraser portion of the pencil. A prompt will ask if you wish to regenerate the model now.

✓ **NOTE:** *This prompt appears just once per model-editing session. If you choose Yes, TriSpectives will load all data-*

base information about the model. You will see several messages in the status area as the IntelliShape model is regenerated. If you choose No, the software will retain the facet model information.

2. If you have not done so already, choose Yes.

After the model is regenerated, you will be able to isolate the four different model components by clicking at various spots on the model. Note the parts of the pencil: the tip, wood, body and eraser/holder. Using surface feature techniques, the designer of this model was able to make simple geometry look more complicated.

Pencil with one of four component IntelliShapes highlighted.

Object Properties

In TriSpectives, all objects consist of elements which can be altered. These elements are known as properties. Object properties fall into three basic categories: shape, model, and style.

Shape Properties

Both 2D and 3D objects are used for design, although 3D objects have more detail than 2D objects. Properties for each category are accessed through separate dialog boxes.

IntelliShape Properties

You will use the IntelliShape Properties dialog box to work with IntelliShapes you have created and models consisting of many IntelliShapes. To access the IntelliShape Properties dialog, complete the following steps.

1. Verify that the Edit IntelliShapes button is depressed.

2. Click on a 3D shape with the right mouse button. Select IntelliShape Properties from the pop-up menu. Note the nine tabs in the dialog box.

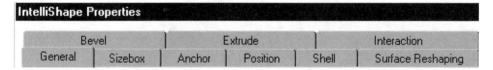

IntelliShape Properties dialog box.

- The *General* tab contains a field listing links to other shapes in the scene. When shapes are linked, they share the same database. This means that a change in one of the linked shapes will also occur in all other shapes to which it is linked.

- The *Sizebox, Anchor, Position,* and *Interaction* tabs are comparable to their counterparts in the 2D shapes dialog box.

- The *Shell* tab relates to the Shell feature in 3D modeling, which deals with hollow areas inside of a model. Shell tab options will change according to the type of shape you are editing.

- The *Surface Reshaping* tab allows you to add taper-ing, end capping, and end matching features to an In-telliShape. Like the Shell tab, the Surface Reshaping tab changes to reflect the model creation technique.

- The *Bevel* tab allows you to add bevels (chamfers and fillets) to groups of edges using entered values, and re-tains the values of such features.

- The final tab is labeled either Extrude, Spin, Sweep, or Lofting, according to the type of shape being edit-ed. It relates to the geometry used to create 3D shapes.

You can access most of the information contained in a model through dialog boxes. However, tools that make editing even eas-ier are also available, as seen in Chapters 3 and 4.

2D Shape Properties

To access the 2D Shape Properties dialog box, follow the steps below.

1. Create a simple 2D object as outlined earlier in this chapter. Click on the object with the right mouse button.

2. Select 2D Shape Properties from the pop-up menu to open the dialog box shown in the next illustration.

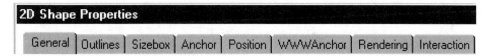

3. Note the eight tabs in the dialog box. Each represents a different feature (aspect) of the shape.

- The *General* tab allows you to rename a shape. This is very helpful when working with a large number of objects in a single scene or with many shapes in a sin-gle model.

- The *Outlines* tab contains detailed information about a shape's geometry. To explore this tab, click on the Show Formulas button while verifying that the Auto Size box is checked. Note that all shape geometry is connected by default to the size of the total shape. Therefore, when you resize the total shape, the geometry making up that shape changes proportionally.

- The *Sizebox* tab lets you set a shape's overall sizing behavior. The tab contains check boxes which allow you to turn Sizebox features on or off. The Aspect lock will lock shape dimensions together, forcing them to change together. The Sizebox tab also lets you set resizing behavior of an object in space.

- The *Anchor* tab lets you set specific anchoring attributes to control how shapes relate to other shapes in the environment. By setting attributes through the Anchor Tab, an object's anchor can attach to the surface, edge, or vertex of another object, and will orient itself perpendicularly to the neighboring surface. Positioning two objects in relation to one another is simplified through the use of anchors.

- The *Position* tab allows you to control precisely the positioning of a shape within a scene. Both translational and rotational positions can serve as input.

✓ **NOTE:** *Anchors are assigned at the shape, model and group levels, each one independent of the other. When you edit the properties of an IntelliShape, model, or group, the meaning of position will be different. IntelliShape position within a model reflects the distance from the IntelliShape anchor to the model anchor. Model and group positions reflect the location relative to the scene center.*

- *WWW Anchor* embedding is used when writing Web pages.

- The *Rendering* tab controls the ability to turn rendering features on and off for individual objects.
- The *Interaction* tab controls the behavior of an object after you double-click on it, drop it into a scene, or drag it with the mouse.

Model Properties

Like shapes, you can access model properties through dialog boxes. In TriSpectives, all 3D objects are considered models. Objects brought in from other modeling software will become facet models, whereas models created within TriSpectives will be comprised of IntelliShapes. Most objects imported from other modeling softwares will become facet models. The exceptions are IGES models imported as a single surface, and STEP or ACIS models imported as IntelliShapes. The dialog box for TriSpectives models is accessed by the same method, but you must first verify that neither of the two edit buttons on the 3D Shapes toolbar is depressed.

✓ **NOTE:** *When you change the size box dimensions of a model comprised of several IntelliShapes, the dimensions of each IntelliShape change proportionally.*

Style Properties

You can control model and shape surface appearance (style) with SmartPaint. To access SmartPaint, click on an object with the right mouse button and select SmartPaint from the pop-up menu. The mode you were in when you selected SmartPaint (either Model Edit mode or Edit Surfaces and Edges mode) will determine which surfaces are affected by your SmartPaint work. The following illustration shows an example of surfaces edited with SmartPaint.

Using the SmartPaint tool, surface appearances can be applied to an entire model (left), or selected surfaces (right).

✓ **NOTE:** *The SmartPaint menu will not appear unless the Edit IntelliShapes button is deselected.*

To apply surface appearance properties to several surfaces, click on the Edit Surfaces and Edges button on the 3D Shapes toolbar. With the <Shift> key depressed, select the surfaces you wish to change. With the right mouse button, click on one of the selected surfaces and choose SmartPaint from the pop-up menu. Tabs in the SmartPaint Properties dialog box are described below.

- The *Color* tab provides options for quickly changing the color and texture of surfaces.

✓ **NOTE:** *TriSpectives has many texture options. They can be found in the* Images *subdirectory wherever TriSpectives is installed on your system. Instructions on using settings for textures are presented in Chapter 5.*

- The *Finish* tab offers options that control the way light reacts with your object. Twelve predefined finishes help you make choices quickly.

- The *Transparency* tab gives models glass or glasslike characteristics. The Index of Refraction slider will control the way in which light bends when it passes through an object.

- The *Bumps* tab creates the appearance of bumps on surfaces through the use of preset textures and images.

- The *Reflection* tab can be used to create the appearance of a mirror causing surfaces to reflect other objects in the scene. Images outside the scene can also be reflected.

- The *Decal* tab is used to add images to the surface of objects similar to the result achieved when applying a sticker to a surface.

- *Emission* creates the impression that a model is giving off light.

Design Session

In this design session, you will use object properties to enhance the model initiated in Chapter 1. If you saved the catalog from Chapter 1, open the file now. If you did not choose to save, open *INSIDE.tsc* from the *Inside* catalog on the companion CD.

Inserting a Model into a New Scene

1. Open the catalog from Chapter 1. Open a new scene by choosing File | New from the menu bar.

2. TriSpectives allows you to use a pre-existing scene to establish defaults. Because you have not yet created a scene with preferred defaults, select the Blank Scene. Click on OK.

3. Select Format | Units and set the units to inches. Click on OK.

4. Drag and drop the *Concept* model into the scene.

Edit the Existing Model

1. Click on the Edit IntelliShapes button on the 3D Shapes toolbar. Click on the top surface of the model and then click on Yes to regenerate the model. When regeneration is complete, right-click on the top surface and select IntelliShape Properties from the pop-up menu.

2. Select the Bevel tab, choose End Section Edges, click on Blend, and enter a value of *0.25* for the Radius. Click on OK.

3. Deselect the shape by clicking in a blank part of the scene. The bevel applied to your model should be visible. Zoom in on the top front corner of the model using the Window Zoom to examine the bevel.

4. Click on the lower step of the table top with the right mouse button. Select IntelliShape Properties from the pop-up menu. Select the Bevel tab, choose End Section Edges, click on Blend, and enter a value of *0.25* for the Radius. Click on OK. Both surfaces should now have a rounded edge.

5. Right-click on the top surface. Repeat step 4, except choose All Intersecting Edges instead of End Section Edges to blend the two surfaces.

Bevels applied to the top edges of the conceptual model to give it an antique look.

6. Repeat steps 1 through 5 for the table base. You may have to experiment to get the starting, ending, and intersecting edges correct.

Finished beveled table top and base.

7. Verify that the Edit IntelliShapes button tool is not selected. Save the model by dragging and dropping it into your personal catalog.

8. When the thumbnail sketch of the object appears, click on the name and rename it *Enhanced*.

Organizing Tools

Using Catalogs

Catalogs are an easy way to build sets of objects that can be reused over and over, either within a single project or over the span of several projects. TriSpectives provides several useful catalogs; you can also create your own catalogs or add objects to existing catalogs, as in the previous exercise.

Catalog Sets

Catalogs can be grouped into sets for easy access, or organized according to personal preference. For instance, you may want to create a separate group for various applications, such as modeling 3D parts, animation and lighting effects, or applying finishing touches to your models. When you are ready to start a new task, simply open the corresponding catalog set and the tools will be readily available. To view pre-existing catalog sets, proceed to the following steps.

1. Select Catalogs | Catalog Sets from the menu bar.

2. Double-click on the Default catalog set. When the default catalogs have been loaded, click on Done. Take a moment to examine the objects in each catalog.

Take the following steps to create a group of catalogs for use in creating visually rich screen shots.

1. Select Catalog Sets from the Catalogs menu.

2. Select the default file, and click on Edit. Change the catalog set name to *Visuals*.

3. Remove all catalogs except Backdrop, Colors, Decals, Surfaces, and Textures. Click on OK.

✓ **NOTE:** *Objects can be easily deleted from a catalog by clicking on them with the right mouse button and then choosing Delete from the pop-up menu.*

4. Verify that *Visuals* is selected, and then click on Open. Note that TriSpectives simultaneously closes all previous catalogs and opens only those within the new set. Click on Done.

Scenes

Multiple scenes can remain open simultaneously. This can be convenient if, for instance, you want to use one scene for creating parts and another for assemblies. Because you can save scenes, you can also use TriSpectives as a 3D presentation tool.

3
Creating and Editing Models

To expand your range of design skills, this chapter focuses on creating more complex models. Topics include adding IntelliShapes to existing models, creating groups of shapes and models, attaching shapes to each other through anchors and attachment points, and aligning surfaces, edges and intersection features. The chapter closes with discussion on using the Triball tool to move and locate shapes.

Complex 3D Models

Simple 3D models, such as blocks and cylinders, have only one geometric shape; most other models are more complex. To render more complex models realistically, material must be removed from existing shapes or new shapes must be added. There are two ways to create complex models in TriSpectives.

Creating Complex Models with IntelliShapes

Using IntelliShapes is often the most convenient method of creating complex models. In model building, IntelliShapes relate to one another through anchor properties, which control, for example, whether a shape is placed on the point, edge, or face of another shape within a model. Follow the exercise below for a demonstration.

1. Open a new scene by selecting File | New from the menu bar.

2. Use the Format | Units menu selection to set the units to centimeters.

3. Drag a block shape from the Shapes catalog into the scene.

4. Find the H Cylinder shape in the catalog and drop it onto the center of the right block face.

Adding the H Cylinder feature to the block shape.

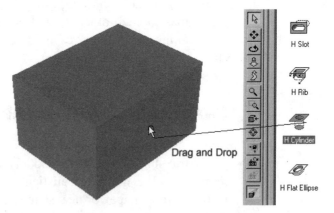

5. Turn on Sizebox dimensions by selecting View | Sizebox Dimensions from the menu bar.

6. Click on the block away from the hole, so that the yellow Sizebox is highlighted. The Sizebox dimensions should be visible.

7. Click on the 150 dimension with the right mouse button, and then select the Edit Sizebox button. Change the length value to *300*. Click on OK.

Note that the hole remained in the middle of the right face. This is because the hole feature is now connected to the block feature.

Block with changed dimensions.

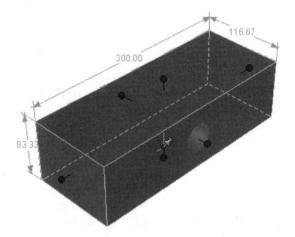

⚹ **TIP:** *To understand the relationship of the shapes in the model illustrated above, click on the hole so that the yellow IntelliShapes Sizebox is highlighted. Click on the hole with the right mouse button. Select IntelliShape Properties from the pop-up menu and then click on the Position tab. Click on Show Formulas and note that each of the values shows SOLVE(Faceconstraint).*

All shapes in a model share the properties applied to the model as a whole. To alter one of the IntelliShapes within the model, simply select it.

Creating Models with Groups

You can also build models by combining groups of shapes and models into larger groups. Groups have the same positioning features as models, and properties applied to a group of shapes will be applied to all shapes or models within the group. Working with groups can also simplify the process of moving many models simultaneously. This is illustrated in the following exercise, in which an office is rearranged so the desk faces the window.

1. Select File | Open from the menu bar and double-click on the *Office.tmd* file located in the *Inside* directory on the companion CD.

2. Click on the desk. A gray highlight should appear.

3. Hold down the <Shift> key and select the in-box, lamp, computer, and chair.

4. Choose Shape | Group from the menu bar. A yellow highlight should appear around all the objects selected.

5. Click on the TriBall positioning tool on the Editing toolbar. By selecting the topmost grip on the TriBall, you limit the model's rotation to the vertical axis. Position the cursor over the topmost grip until a hand appears, and then click on the grip. The vertical axis should be highlighted in yellow. If you move inside the TriBall boundary, the cursor will change to a hand with a rotation arrow under it.

TriBall positioning tool.

Topmost TriBall grip.

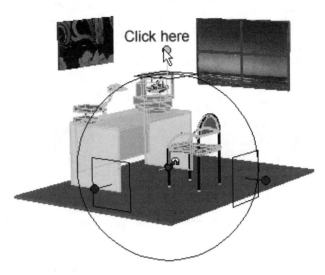

6. Starting at the right side of the TriBall, click and hold down the mouse button, then slowly drag to the left while keeping the cursor on the surface of the globe as though you are guiding a ball. The group of models will rotate, and numbers will appear on the screen indicating the rotation angle. The numbers will remain when you release the mouse button.

7. Right-click on the lower left number. Select the Edit Value button and enter a value of *90* for the angle of rotation. Click on OK. The office is now oriented toward the window, but the furniture is floating above the floor. Fortunately, it is easy to move within a plane using the TriBall.

8. Position the mouse over the uppermost square on the TriBall until the cursor turns into a four-way arrow, indicating you are about to perform a planar move. In this instance, the move is along the plane parallel to the floor. Click on the square and slowly drag until the furniture seems correctly positioned over the floor.

Select button.

9. Choose the Select tool from the Camera toolbar. Click in a blank area of the scene to deselect the group and observe the new view.

Multiple objects repositioned by creating a group.

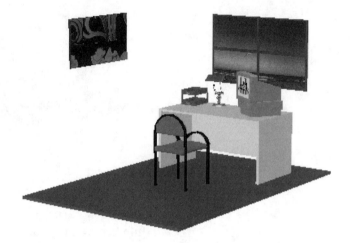

Attaching Shapes

All shapes and models created in TriSpectives have anchors that control the way they relate to other objects in the scene.

Attachment Points

One method of orienting models to each other is through attachment points. Attachment points tell models where to snap to and at what angle to orient with other attachment points. Take the following steps to observe the method in practice.

1. Open a new scene by selecting File | New from the menu bar. Drag a block shape from the Shapes catalog into the scene. Click on the block until a blue highlight appears.

2. Select Insert | Attachment Point from the menu bar and click on the top center of the block. A green orientation marker should appear on the block. Drag a cylinder shape from the Shapes catalog and drop it onto the new attachment point.

3. Edit the parameters of the attachment point to see how the shapes are currently relating to one another. Click on the block so that the blue highlight appears, and then right-click and select Model Properties.

4. Click on the Attachment Points tab. In the Orientation area, enter *1* in the L: field, and *120* in the By this angle field.

Adjusting the orientation of the attachment point.

> **Attachment Points**
>
> ┌─ Orientation ─────────────────
> │ Rotate around this axis:
> │   L: [1   ]
> │   W: [0   ]
> │   H: [0   ]
> │ By this angle:
> │   [120.00   ]

5. Click on OK. The cylinder you dropped onto the block earlier in the exercise is now repositioned.

*Cylinder repositioned
on the block.*

Aligning Surfaces

Another way to join objects is to attach one object to the face of another. The anchor of the second object will typically continue to point away from the surface of the first object. Perform the following steps to see how this process works.

1. Drag and drop the sphere shape from the Shapes catalog into the scene. Verify that the Edit IntelliShapes button is not selected.

2. Drag and drop a cylinder onto the surface of the sphere. Note how the cylinder orients itself pointing away from the sphere. The point of attachment is the anchor of the cylinder. The anchor of the cylinder points away from the sphere, meaning that the new shape's position is normal to the surface of the first shape.

Cylinder joined to sphere in default (normal) position.

3. The magnet at the anchor of the cylinder indicates the cylinder shape is constrained to slide along surfaces only. Click on the cylinder and drag it to a new location. Note how the cylinder slides along the surface of the sphere, and that it remains normal to the surface at all times.

A mode of attachment similar to Slide Along Surfaces is Attach to Surface. The difference between the two methods is apparent only when you move or modify the shape to which you are attaching, and only when the shapes belong to the same model. Attach to Surface creates a parametric relationship between two shapes so that when they are altered, the point of attachment retains the same relationship. Follow the steps below for an illustration.

1. Turn the Edit IntelliShapes button on and drag another cylinder shape from the Shapes catalog onto the sphere. The new cylinder takes on the same color as the sphere, indicating that they are part of the same model.

New cylinder attached to the surface of the sphere.

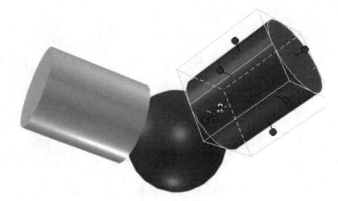

The anchor now shows a magnet with two lightning bolts under it, indicating the new shape is attached to the surface of the sphere. If you try to move the new cylinder, it will behave just as the first cylinder did, sliding along the surface of the sphere. The difference is apparent only when you modify the sphere to which the cylinders are anchored.

2. Click on the sphere until the yellow Sizebox appears, then drag one of the handles outward to enlarge the sphere.

3. Release the handle. Note that the first cylinder is no longer anchored to the sphere surface. However, the second cylinder has moved with the sphere surface to the new diameter because it is truly attached to the surface.

The same pattern of relationship would apply if you moved the sphere to a new location. The first cylinder would remain stationary while the second cylinder moved with the sphere.

4. Click on the red cylinder. Move the mouse cursor over the center of the cylinder anchor until the dot changes from red to yellow. Click on the dot with the right mouse button.

5. Click on Move Freely in Space in the pop-up menu. Move the cylinder around in space. The behavior of the shape has changed because you have changed the anchor mode.

6. Click on the anchor dot again with the right mouse button. Select Fixed Position. Note the thumbtack that pops up on top of the shape anchor.

7. Try to move the cylinder. As you may have expected, the shape is immovable.

✓ **NOTE:** *Attach to Surface and Slide Along Surfaces give shapes within a model the ability to attach to other shapes within the same model. Slide Along Surfaces allows entire models to slide over the available surfaces of any other model.*

Aligning to Edges and Points

There are several ways to align new shapes brought into a scene. They may be aligned on surfaces, along edges, or at certain key points on existing shapes in a scene. These points include the centers of planar faces, midpoints of linear and arc edges, circular and arc geometry centers, and all vertices.

Fine Tuning Model Appearance

An easy way to improve model appearance is to add *bevels* (blends or chamfers). Most real life objects do not have perfectly square corners; for this reason, you will probably want to use bevels to eliminate such corners from 3D models. The Design Session in Chapter 2 demonstrated how to apply bevels to the edges of a table.

A *radius blend*, sometimes referred to as a fillet, results when two pieces of metal are welded together. In TriSpectives, use a 3D blend when you want to blend two shapes together smoothly or round off the corners of a model.

Chamfers are similar to blends, but are straight rather than round. Chamfers can add aesthetically pleasing features to models. A chamfer and blend are illustrated in the following figure.

Simple cube with one edge blended and another chamfered.

✓ **NOTE:** *Both types of bevels can be added to edges or vertices by selecting the desired edges while the Edit Surfaces and Edges button is depressed. While holding down the <Shift> key, select several edges. Right-click on an edge to access the Bevel Edges dialog box.*

➥ **TIP:** *When applying multiple bevels to a model, begin with the largest bevel and work down to the smallest. This practice will prevent conflicts.*

Moving Shapes

As discussed in Chapter 2, TriSpectives offers several different ways of moving shapes, each appropriate in different situations.

Freehand

Dragging and dropping models or shapes is simple, but the degree of precision is controlled only by your eye. Anchor constraints may also restrict ease of movement to ensure important relationships are maintained. In addition, you will probably need to frequently rotate the scene to understand the true location of objects.

Position Parameters

The most accurate way of moving objects is through position parameters. However, this method can be cumbersome if you have not determined final positions, or would like to eyeball the move before you set the final decimal place.

> ✓ **NOTE:** *Position parameters are located in the Model Properties and IntelliShape Properties dialog boxes.*

TriBall

The TriBall is one of TriSpectives' most versatile tools. You can use it for translational and rotational moves.

Translational Moves

Translational moves can be accomplished along one of the three planes related to any part or model. To move an object, click on a plane of the TriBall and drag the object to a new location. You can perform a translation along a single axis by clicking on an axis and dragging the object to a new position.

Rotational Moves

Rotational moves can be made in three ways.

❑ Rotational movements about all three axes simultaneously can be made by clicking within the Triball interior and dragging the object to a new position. This method offers little control, but may be appropriate when an approximation is all you need.

❑ To rotate about an axis that extends toward you from the screen, move the cursor to the TriBall's circular border. The border will change to yellow, and the cursor will become a rotating arrow. Next, click and drag on the border. This method is handy if flat faces coordinate with the desired rotational axes, because you can first orient the scene with the Look At tool.

❑ A third method of rotating objects is to first click on one of the axes and then rotate about that axis, as illustrated earlier in this chapter. This method offers the highest level of control while permitting you to get to an approximate location in a freehand manner.

Additional built-in capabilities of the TriBall are discussed in subsequent chapters.

Saving Models

Save your work often during the model building process. Use the File | Save menu selection to save the current scene and all models within the scene. To save a model for multiple usage in the same project or for use in later projects, save it to a catalog.

Creating and Editing Shapes

This chapter focuses both on tailoring the program to suit your needs and on new ways of creating and editing shapes. Topics include changing default options, tools for creating 2D geometry, the use of 2D geometry in creating 3D shapes, and removing material from models using "negative shapes." The Shapes catalog is also explored in greater detail.

Changing Default Settings

Default settings for units, grids, and working environment options can be altered. Alterations are discussed in the following sections.

Linear and Angular Units

Default linear and angular units can be changed within a scene by selecting Format | Units. If you have already created parts using one set of units and then switch to another set, the size of the shape will not change. Instead, the new units, along with the converted values, will be displayed in all editing dialog boxes as demonstrated in the following example.

1. Open a new scene. Under the View menu, verify that the Grid, Sizebox Dimensions, and Position Dimensions are turned on.

2. Drag and drop a block shape from the Shapes catalog into the scene. You will see two position dimensions that show the distance from the model anchor to the origin of the scene.

3. Select Format | Units from the menu bar to open the Units dialog box. Change the linear dimensions to inches. The display will update with the new units and values.

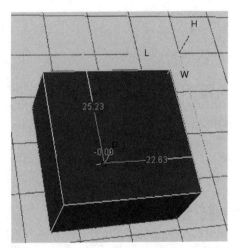 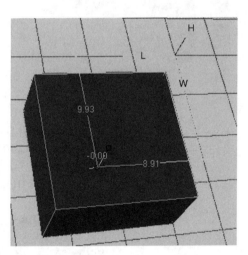

Block shape dimensions changed from centimeters (left) to inches (right).

Switching back and forth between two types of units can cause confusion and invite errors. To reduce such problems, the right portion of the status bar notes units currently in use.

⇨ **TIP:** *To view the units indicator, verify that the Status bar selection in the View menu is checked.*

Grid Settings

The Grid dialog box controls the behavior of scene grids. If you have determined the size of the world you want to work in, you can set the grid default to your preference. Remember that units for grid settings will reflect currently active units.

To set a preferred default size for new parts, select Format | Default Size from the menu bar. Note, however, that changing the default size will not affect catalog shapes with predefined sizes or shapes in the Advshapes catalog.

Working Options

You can alter other default settings with the Tools | Options menu selection. The Options dialog box contains the five tabs described below.

❏ The *General* tab controls the following working options:

- Display of selected dialogs and wizards
- Number of decimal places dialog boxes and dimensions will display
- Size of the area in pixels a mouse click will cover
- Number of "undo" steps TriSpectives will retain
- Whether to save texture image data with a scene file.

✗ **WARNING:** *Due to computer memory limitations, employing a large number of undo steps may cause difficulties. If you find that TriSpectives crashes or runs slowly, try reducing the number of undo steps.*

❏ The *Models* tab in the Options dialog box covers the default behavior of models. Options are described below.

- Drop TriSpectives models into a scene as facet or IntelliShape models

- Attachment behavior of new shapes dropped onto existing models
- Regenerate a model automatically either after a change is completed or when it is deselected
- Saving approximate or exact surface data
- Alter the behavior of SmartPaint textures when dropped onto a model
- Whether to display model edges as colored lines

❏ The *Directories* tab allows you to decide which directories searched for working files, templates, and image files.

❏ The *Mouse* tab allows you to choose how the middle button of a three-button mouse behaves in TriSpectives. Other software normally used to drive the mouse must be disabled before the TriSpectives behavior can activate.

❏ The *Color* tab allows you to select default colors for a wide variety of highlights, tools, and model features.

> ✗ **WARNING:** *This book assumes you are using default properties for display settings. If you change the defaults, you may have trouble following exercises later in this book.*

Inside the Shapes Catalog

As mentioned in Chapter 1, predefined IntelliShapes are stored in the Shapes catalog. These shapes are great time-savers in model design. If you have not explored all the predefined shapes available to you, now would be a good time to do so. See also the *Advshaps.tsc* catalog.

The descriptive names in the Shapes catalog require some explanation. Any shape using an extruded method to create geometry has a simple descriptive name, such as *Block, Cylinder,* or *Poly.* Shapes using a spin method either have simple descriptive names or start with the prefix *S.* All lofted shapes have an *L* prefix. Swept shapes have an *SW* prefix. Negative shapes follow all these rules *and* have an additional prefix of *H*.

Extruded, spin, lofted, swept, and negative shapes from the Shapes catalog.

IntelliShapes

All entries in the Shapes catalog are IntelliShapes. IntelliShapes enhance work efficiency because they do not have to be regenerated before editing, and can be dragged and dropped onto existing scenes while working in Edit IntelliShapes mode. The size of IntelliShapes dropped from the Shapes and Advanced Shapes catalogs is determined by the default size setting.

Negative IntelliShapes

Negative IntelliShapes are used to remove material from a model, rather than add material to it. Almost all negative shapes in the catalog are simply inversions of positive shapes. Follow the steps below to change a positive shape into a negative one, and then use it to remove material from another shape.

1. Drag a block shape from the Shapes catalog into the scene. With Edit IntelliShapes mode turned off, drag a cylinder shape from the Shapes catalog to the center of one of the block's faces. Once in the scene, the cylinder should be a different color than the block, indicating that it is a separate model.

2. Click on the cylinder until the yellow highlight with sizebox handles appears. Then reduce the cylinder's diameter by dragging one of the side handles toward the center.

3. Right-click on the IntelliShape while it is still highlighted. Select Flip Extrude Direction in the pop-up menu. Click in a blank part of the scene to deselect the shape.

4. Click on the cylinder until the blue highlight appears. Select Shape | Set Operation, and then select Remove Material. Click on OK.

5. Deselect the model again. This is necessary so that you can join the two models using a Boolean operation, in which the outcome depends on the order of model selection.

6. Click on the block until the blue highlight appears. Hold down the <Shift> key and click on the cylinder to select it as well.

7. Use the Shape | Boolean menu selection to remove the cylinder material from the block. The result is a block with a cylinder-shaped hole, as seen in the next illustration.

Block with a cylinder-shaped hole.

The method described above is not the only way to create a cylindrical hole. Other easier ways are explained later in this chapter. However, the exercise you just performed illustrates the importance of negative shapes in model creation. The use of negative shapes is also a convenient and effective way to create a mold, as shown in the following illustration.

Piggy bank mold created through a Boolean operation.

Creating New IntelliShapes

All 3D shapes contain at least one 2D cross section. For this reason, you will often use 2D editing tools to create new 3D shapes. In this section, 2D tools will be employed in conjunction with each of the four 3D modeling techniques.

Extruding

One of the simplest 3D modeling methods, extruding requires only a single cross section, which can be simple or complex. Cylinders, cubes, and slabs, for example, are all made by extruding. Take the following steps to create the simple extruded model shown in the next illustration.

A simple extruded model.

Extrude Shape button.

1. Open a new scene by selecting File | New from the menu bar. If the 2D Technical Editing toolbar is not active, select View | Toolbars and click on the 2D Technical Editing box.

✓ **NOTE:** *The 2D Technical Drawing toolbar loads automatically when you start a 2D modeling command, if it is not already active.*

2. Select the Extrude Shape tool from the 3D Shapes toolbar, and then click in the scene to access the Extrude Shape Wizard. When prompted, enter *1.0* for the length to be extruded and click on Next.

3. Because the simple extrusion is the first shape in this model, it must be given Stand Alone status.

4. Click on Next and select Yes to display the grid. Enter *1* for both vertical and horizontal spacing. Click on the Default box to set these entries as the default setting.

5. Click on Finish. The Edit Cross-Section dialog box will appear.

6. Select the Circle Radius tool on the 2D Technical Drawing toolbar. Click at the center of the cross section grid for the first point, and then at any other point to complete the circle.

7. Choose the Select tool and right-click on the radius dimension of the circle. Select Edit Value.

Edit Value button displayed after a dimension has been selected.

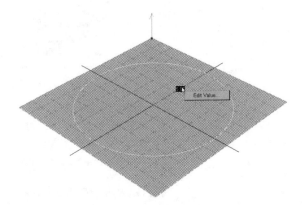

✓ **NOTE:** *If you do not see the dimension value for the radius, you may need to make curve dimensions visible. Simply select View | Curve Dimensions from the menu bar and restart this exercise.*

8. Enter a radius of *5.0* and click on OK. Click on the Finish Shape button in the Edit Cross-Section dialog box.

To complete the model, take the following steps.

1. Turn on Edit IntelliShapes and once again choose the Extrude Shape button. This time, however, drop the shape at the center of the existing shape. A green dot will appear when you are on center.

Fit Scene button.

Project Edges to Drawing Grid button.

Bezier button.

Selecting points for a Bezier curve.

2. Enter a distance of *0.5* and click on Next. Because you will want to remove material, click on the appropriate box and then click on Finish.

3. Use the Look At tool to orient the scene, and then the Fit Scene tool to center it.

4. Select Project Edges to Drawing Grid on the 2D Technical Editing toolbar. Click on the outline of the disk you just created. Choose the Select tool and change the radius value to *4.8*. Click on OK.

5. Select the Bezier tool and move the cursor over the center top point on the circle. Click to place the first point of the curve. Place a second point at approximately *2.0, 2.0*, and a third point at *–2.0, –2.0*.

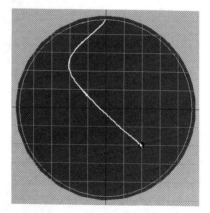

6. Finish the curve by double-clicking at the bottom center of the circle.

✓ **NOTE:** *It is important that cross sections be continuous. All red dots will disappear as a signal you have made the cross section continuous and are ready to finish the operation.*

7.   Select the Trim Curve Between Curves tool and click on
one side of the circle. You should see a green asterisk,
indicating the curve that you wish to cut. To trim away
half the circle, click on the Bezier curve near the top of
the circle, and then again near the bottom of the circle.

8.   Choose the Select tool to view the results of the trim
operation, which should match the next illustration.

Trim operation results.

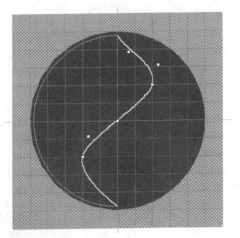

9.   Adjust the control points of the Bezier curve until you
are pleased with the way the shape looks. Select Finish
from the Edit Cross-Section dialog box.

*Adjusting control points
of the Bezier curve.*

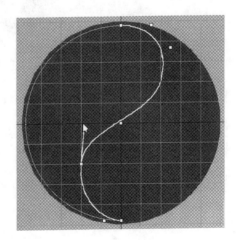

10. Using the Orbit Camera tool, rotate the 3D model to examine your results. You may want to save it by dropping it into the catalog.

Spinning

The spin shape method of model creation spins a single cross section around a rotational axis. It is not necessary to spin a curve 360 degrees to use this tool. Most rolled and lathe-created objects (such as spun pottery) are most easily modeled using the spin shape method.

Use the spin shape method in the following steps to create the shape below.

Spun cup and saucer without a handle.

1. Select File | New to open a new scene. Click on OK to accept the default scene preferences.

Spin Shape button.

2. Select the Spin Shape button from the 3D Shapes toolbar and click in the scene. The Spin Shape Wizard will default to a spin angle of 360 degrees, which is acceptable. Because you are not attaching this shape to a model, the default orientation is also acceptable.

3. Click twice on Next. Set the grid lines at *1* for both the horizontal and vertical spacing. Select the Default box to set default settings.

4. Click on Finish. The 2D drawing grid will appear in the scene. Use the Look At and Fit Scene tools to bring the drawing grid into orientation.

5. Right-click on the grid and select Snap from the pop-up menu. Set the snap angle increment to five degrees and then click OK.

6. Using the Polyline tool, create a shape similar to the one illustrated below. Be careful to ensure that the end-points near the vertical axis (see the arrow in the following illustration) lie on the construction line. Because of the choices you made in the Spin Shape Wizard, the vertical axis is the axis around which the cross section will be spun.

Polyline tool.

A 2D cross section, the first step in creating a spun model.

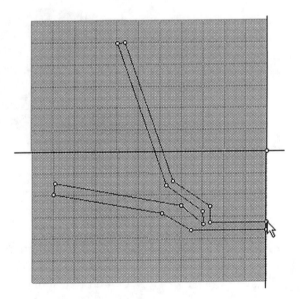

✓ **NOTE:** *Spin shape profiles do not have to be closed. The system will project the end points horizontally back to the axis, thereby creating a straight edge.*

7. Click on Finish Shape in the Edit Cross-Section dialog box. Your image should match the image illustrated at the beginning of this exercise.

Sweeping

Swept shapes have a single cross section and can be understood as extrusions along a curved path. The sweep shape method is commonly used to create tube-like objects. Follow the steps below to create a handle for the cup using the sweep shape method.

Sweep Shape button.

1. Choose the Sweep Shape button on the 3D Shapes toolbar, and then click in a blank part of the scene.

2. Select Away From the Surface as the orientation. Click on Next. Then select Bezier Curve as the type of sweep path and click on Next.

3. Because you started this model by clicking in a blank part of the scene, the default is Stand Alone. Click on Next and set grid lines to *1*, as indicated in previous exercises. Click on Finish.

4. Orient the scene using the Look At tool, and then zoom in on the grid using the Window Zoom tool.

Follow the next series of steps to create the cross section for the swept shape.

Rectangle tool.

1. Use the Rectangle tool to draw a *1.0* by *1.0* box. Deselect the Rectangle tool.

Drawing a rectangle.

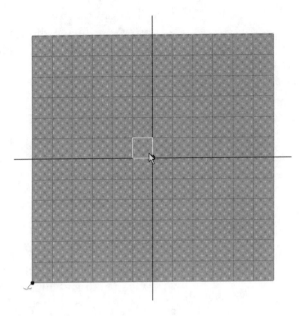

Smooth 2D
Corners button.

2. Choose Edit | Select All Curves from the menu bar. Click on the Smooth 2D Corners button. Enter a value of *0.10* for the radius. Click on OK.

3. Click on Finish Shape. A new dialog box entitled Edit Sweep Path replaces the previous one. If you use the Orbit Camera to turn the scene, a new drawing grid will also be visible. Use the Look At tool to orient the scene to the new grid.

4. Adjust the control points of the Bezier curve so that the final shape appears as shown in the next illustration.

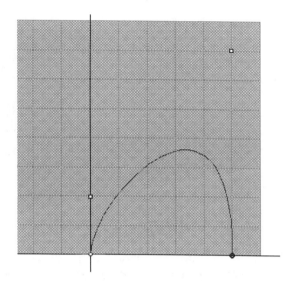

Cross section and sweep curve for cup handle.

5. Click on Finish Shape. You will now see a cup with a handle, although the handle is not appropriately placed.

The placement of the handle is inappropriate because clicking on a blank area earlier in this exercise placed the handle at an arbitrary, rather than exact, point. To reposition the handle, complete the following steps.

1. Select the TriBall tool. Move and rotate the handle until it is in the correct place on the cup.

2. When the handle is positioned correctly, hold down the <Shift> key and select both models. Perform a Boolean addition by selecting Shapes | Boolean from the menu bar. The result is the cup and saucer pictured below.

*Cup, handle, and saucer
created using the spin
shape and sweeping
methods.*

Lofting

Lofting is perhaps the most interesting and challenging of model creation methods, and always involves at least two cross sections. With lofting you can create many free-form shapes and abstract looking models. However, it requires more input and time than other model creation methods.

Take the following steps to create the vase shown below.

*Vase created using
lofting method.*

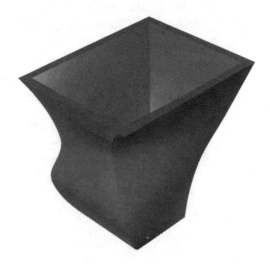

*Loft Shape
button.*

1. Open a new file. Select Loft Shape from the 3D Shapes toolbar, and then click in the scene.

2. Accept the default of four cross sections by clicking on Next. Set the Cross-section type to Rectangles and the Path type to Straight Line. Click Next twice and set grid lines to *1*, as explained in previous exercises. Click on Finish. The generated model will appear as shown in the next illustration.

*Default loft shape appears
as a rectangular block.*

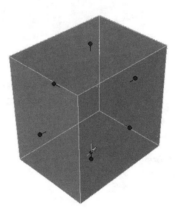

3. When the model has been generated, right-click in the scene and select Rendering. Then set Style to Wireframe and click on OK.

4. Click on the shape until a yellow outline appears. Right-click on the shape and select Show Cross-Sections from the pop-up menu.

5. Right-click on the *1* (one). Select Edit on Grid from the pop-up menu. Right-click on the grid and select Show from the pop-up menu. Turn on Show End Point Positions and click OK.

Grid after selecting Edit on Grid.

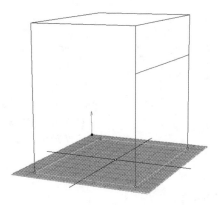

6. Move the four corners of the rectangle so that they form a square. The corners should be located two units from the center of the grid in each direction.

Moving the four corners of the cross section.

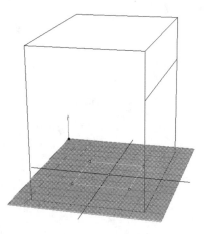

Offset 2D Curves button.

7. Select Edit I Select All Curves from the menu. Click on Offset 2D Curves from the 2D Technical Editing toolbar. Enter a value of *0.5* in the Distance field, and toggle on Flip Direction. Click on OK.

8. Click on Next Section. Now, repeat steps 6 and 7 for each of the three remaining cross sections. Input the corner point positions as listed below.

- Section 2: (4,3), (4,-3), (-2,-1), (-3,2)
- Section 3: (3,1), (4,-2), (-4,-3), (-4,3)
- Section 4: (5,4), (5,-4), (-5,-4), (-5,4)

➡ **TIP:** *An alternate way to edit point locations is to right-click on a point and then select Edit Position from the pop-up menu.*

9. When you have finished editing the cross sections, click on Finish Shape.

Wireframe image of the new lofted shape.

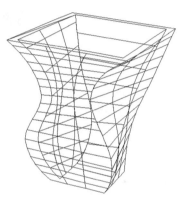

Now you need to cover the hole left by the loft construction. Take the following steps to add a simple extruded shape to the bottom of the vase.

1. Right-click in a blank area of the scene and select Rendering from the pop-up menu. Then select Smooth Shading and click on OK.

2. Select the Edit IntelliShapes button on the 3D Shapes toolbar. Now rotate the scene using the Orbit Camera until you are viewing the small end of the vase. Select the Extrude Shape tool.

3. Click on one corner of the small end of the base. Enter a value of *0.5* for how far the shape should be extruded, and then click on Next.

Selecting a bottom corner of the vase to add an IntelliShape.

4. Select Add Material. Click on Next and verify that the grid lines are set to *1*. Click on Finish. Use the rectangle tool on the 2D Technical Drawing toolbar to draw a square that sufficiently covers the hole.

Adding a base to the lofted vase model.

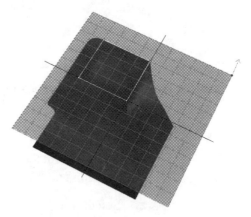

5. Click on Finish Shape to complete the vase, which should resemble the figure at the beginning of this exercise.

5
Applying Colors, Textures, and Effects

Colors, textures, and surface finishes are critical to an object's appearance. Similarly, a viewer is impacted by the background against which an object is presented. This chapter focuses on providing the tools to make the objects and backgrounds in the virtual world almost as colorful and subtle as the physical world. Topics include adding color and texture using SmartPaint and the drag and drop method, and adding surface effects such as decals and bumps.

Colors

Every time you create a model in a new scene it is colored red, the default color. However, you may want to change the color of other models you create to quickly distinguish among them. TriSpectives gives you three ways to change the color of an object, all of them easy to use.

Drag and Drop Colors

The drag and drop method allows you to experiment with different colors without taking the time to access dialog boxes. Simply pick a color from the catalog and drop it onto a model, as illustrated in the steps below.

1. Open a new scene using the File | New menu pick. Verify that the Edit IntelliShapes button is not selected.

2. Verfiy that the Catalog Browser is visible. Click on the *My Catalog* tab. If the catalog is not open, use Catalogs | Open to open it.

3. Drag the *Enhanced* model from the catalog into the scene. If you did not save the model to *My Catalog* while completing Chapter 4, you can retrieve a copy of it from the *Inside* catalog on the companion CD.

4. Open the Colors catalog, if necessary, and select the Colors catalog tab.

5. Right-click in the catalog. Select Small Icons from the pop-up menu.

✓ **NOTE:** *TriSpectives offers more than 200 predefined colors, any of which you can drag and drop onto models.*

6. Select the icon of any color you prefer. Drag and drop the color onto the shape.

✓ **NOTE:** *One advantage of the drag and drop method is that the color can be referred to by name.*

SmartPaint Colors

Another way to add color to an object is with SmartPaint. Although Smart Paint offers a smaller initial palette of colors than the Colors catalog, you can increase available colors by creating custom colors. To create a custom color and add it to the model, complete the following steps.

1. Verify that the Edit buttons on the 3D Shapes toolbar are not depressed. Right-click on the model and select SmartPaint from the pop-up menu.

2. In the dialog box, select More Colors. Note that your choice of colors is slightly expanded.

3. Choose Define Custom Colors from the new dialog box. An even wider range of colors is now offered. Click in the Color Selection box and adjust the vertical slider at the right of the Color dialog box to change the luminescence of a particular color.

4. To use a custom color, click on the Add to Custom Colors button at the bottom of the Color dialog box. When you have chosen a new color, click on this button.

✓ **NOTE:** *You can add up to 16 custom colors per session by repeating the process outlined in steps 3 and 4.*

5. Click on OK. Note that your color does not appear on the default color palette. Click on OK again to exit the SmartPaint Properties dialog box and apply the new color to your model.

✓ **NOTE:** *You cannot save custom colors from one session to another. If you find a custom color that you like, note the values for future use.*

SmartPaint Wizard for Colors

You can also apply colors using the SmartPaint Wizard. The Wizard contains six pages, the first of which you will use in the exercises in this chapter. Other pages and more advanced options will be discussed in Chapter 8. Take the steps below to apply a color with the SmartPaint Wizard.

1. Right-click on the model and select SmartPaint Wizard from the pop-up menu.

2. Click on Colors to access the Color dialog box previously discussed. Choose a color and click on OK to close the Color dialog box.

3. Click on Finish to apply the color.

The SmartPaint Wizard can also be used to add textures, as discussed in the following section.

Applying Textures

Textures add richness and realism to models. A texture is simply an image applied to the surface of a model. However, the way the image is applied or "mapped" onto a model significantly affects its final appearance.

Drag and Drop Textures

Textures can be dragged and dropped onto models in the same way as colors. To explore this method, open the Textures catalog, if necessary, and select the Texture tab. Browse the contents and experiment by dragging several textures onto a model.

SmartPaint Textures

Textures can also be applied using the SmartPaint dialog box. This method provides the highest level of control over the way the texture image is mapped onto the model. Take the following steps for a demonstration.

1. Right-click on the model and select SmartPaint from the pop-up menu. If you applied a texture during the SmartPaint Wizard exercise, the Image Texture bullet in the SmartPaint Properties dialog box will be selected. If it is not selected, select it now.

2. Select Browse Files and locate the *Images* directory.

3. Select the *WalBurl.tif* file and click on Open. Note that a thumbnail image of the new texture appears, and that the Preview shows the image applied to a sphere.

4. Click on the Settings button and set the width and height of the Projected Image to *40*. Click on OK.

5. Drag the dialog box to a spot that allows you to view the result of your work. Click on Apply.

Image Projection

When working with SmartPaint, you can control the way an image is applied to a model. As mentioned earlier, this can affect a model's presentation impact. There are five different applications, some more suitable for certain shapes than others.

- *Automatic* projects an image from six sides of a box toward the model.

- *Slide projector* projects an image onto the model from one angle only.

- *Cylindrical* projects an image onto a cylindrical surface as though the cylinder were unrolled and laid flat. (This does not work well on the ends of a cylinder, however.)

- *Spherical* wraps an image onto a spherical object. This method will also work on other shapes.

- *Natural* projects an image to follow the natural contour of model surfaces. This works best on twisted or other irregular shapes.

To experiment with image projection, follow the steps below.

1. Unless you are already in the SmartPaint dialog, right-click on the model. Select SmartPaint from the pop-up menu.

2. From the center section of the Color tab, choose cylindrical as the Image Projection. Click on Apply. Experiment by changing the projection techniques and clicking on Apply to view the effects.

3. When you are finished exploring, set Image projection to Automatic, and then click on OK.

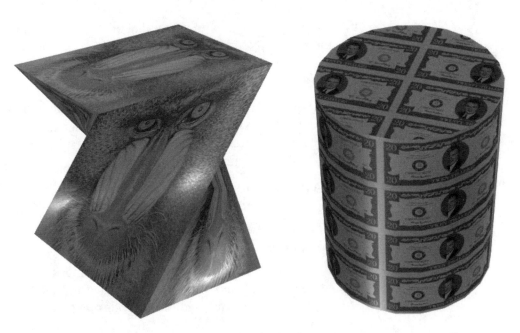

Natural (left) and cylindrical (right) methods of projecting images.

SmartPaint Wizard for Textures

The SmartPaint Wizard is also convenient for applying textures to models. Apply a texture using SmartPaint Wizard with the following steps.

Right-click on the model and select the SmartPaint Wizard from the pop-up menu. Page one offers the choice of 14 textures. Choose a texture and click on Finish to apply.

> ✓ **NOTE 1:** *To choose another texture, click on the Browse button to access the Select Image File dialog box. Locate the preferred file, click to open, and bring it into the Smart-Paint Wizard.*

> ✓ **NOTE 2:** *If a new texture is not visible, right-click in the scene to access the pop-up menu. Verify that Rendering is set to Smooth Shading and that the Show Textures box is selected. If both options are in place, try pressing <Ctrl>+R to initiate rendering.*

Applying Surface Effects

Decals

Decals can add dramatic or decorative effects to models, and can be applied to one or more model surfaces. To illustrate, take the following steps.

1. Because it is best to apply decals to one surface at a time, turn on the Edit Surfaces and Edges button on the 3D Shapes toolbar.

2. Right-click on the top surface of the table model and select SmartPaint from the pop-up menu. Click on the Decal tab. Choose Decal from selected image bullet.

*Move Decal
button.*

3. In the *Images* directory, double-click on the *Arabesq.tif* file and click on OK.

4. To reposition the decal, click on the Move Decal button on the Editing toolbar. Move the Sizebox around to resize and move the decal. The TriBall tool can also be used to reposition the decal.

✓ *NOTE: Outside handles change size. When dragged, the center handle changes positions.*

5. Right-click on the Sizebox. This pop-up menu provides the opportunity to choose a new image projection method, flip the image, fit the image to the model, select a new image file, change the settings in the dialog box, and reset the changes you have made. Click on Fit to Model. Deselect the Move Decal tool.

Table created in Chapter 1 with applied texture and decal (left), and with part of the decal made transparent (right).

You can achieve a different effect by making part of a decal transparent. Your menu choice of black, white, or color pixels will determine which portion of the decal is made transparent. In the example, you will be replacing the dark blue pixels of the decal you just finished placing on the table top.

1. Right-click on the table top and select SmartPaint from the pop-up menu. Click on the Decal tab.

2. Set Type Transparency to See-through. Select "user color pixels" as the material to make transparent.

3. Click on User Color and select Define Custom Colors. To specify the color enter *0* for red and green, and *102* for blue. Select Add to custom colors and click on OK. Click on OK again to apply the modified decal.

4. Deselect the Edit Edges and Surfaces tool. Drag the table into *My Catalog* and rename it *Table*.

✓ **NOTE:** *Decals applied via drag and drop override the surface color. If you wish to keep the surface color for use with a partially transparent decal, you must apply the decal using the SmartPaint Wizard or SmartPaint Properties dialog boxes.*

Bumps

Bumps can also be applied to models to give them a more realistic look. The following example illustrates the method of application.

1. Open the Shapes catalog and drag a sphere shape into the scene. Right-click on the sphere and select Smart-Paint from the pop-up menu.

2. Select the Image Texture bullet, then browse to locate the *Tenisbal.tif* image in the *Images* directory.

3. Set Image projection to Spherical, and then click on Apply to view the result. As illustrated below, what you get looks almost like a tennis ball, but lacks the surface fuzziness.

Tennis ball texture applied to a sphere (left). Bumps applied to tennis ball create fuzzy appearance (right).

4. Click on the Bumps tab and select Make Bumps from Image. Navigate to locate the *Images\Spatter.tif* file, then click on Open. Set Image projection to Spherical for the bumps, and set the Bump height to 5.

✓ **NOTE:** *In order to view bumps, Rendering must be set to Realistic shading.*

5. The ratio of the bumps image to the ball size may not be accurate. To resolve this problem, click on the Settings button. A dialog box specific to the projection method, in this case Spherical, appears. Enter *10* for the Horizontal ratio and the Vertical ratio, and then click on OK. Click on OK again to finish the tennis ball model.

✓ **NOTE:** *The Move Bumps button on the Editing toolbar is also useful for adjusting the appearance of bumps.*

Move Bumps button.

Altering Backgrounds

Many of the methods used to alter the appearance of models can be used to alter backgrounds. You can drag colors, textures, bumps, and decals from catalogs and drop them on the background to create interesting effects. You can also work with the Scene Properties dialog box, as described in the following exercise.

1. Right-click in the scene and select Background from the pop-up menu. The Scene Properties dialog box appears, offering you the option of working with colors or images. Click on the Image Texture bullet.

⊷ **TIP:** *To apply image texture to backgrounds, you can stretch the image to fill the scene and preserve the aspect ratio of the original image file, or fill the scene by repeating the image to create a pattern.*

2. Browse to the *Images* directory, and select the *Stellar1.tif* file. Click on Open, then click on OK to apply. Take a few minutes to explore other backgrounds you might wish to apply to the scene.

6

Creating Technical Documents

This chapter focuses on adding design annotations to models and using TriSpectives to improve the appearance and functionality of technical documents. Topics include the use of SmartDimensions in annotation, creating multiple views of models, exporting models to other CAD programs, embedding specification sheets in a scene using OLE (object linking and embedding), and linking models to spreadsheets.

Annotation

Models are annotated using SmartDimensions. SmartDimensions have three important features. First, they are dynamically linked to a model through directional associativity, meaning that when you change the model, the dimension values also change. Second, SmartDimensions snap to surfaces and surface features. Third, they can be placed between models to specify the distance between them, or you can use SmartDimensions to specify the distance between shapes within a single model. Try adding Smart Dimensions to a model by taking the following steps.

1. Open a new scene by selecting File | New from the menu bar. Add a cylinder from the Shapes Catalog to the new scene. If the Resize Shape dialog box appears, set the shape size to 10 units. Ensure that SmartDimensions are visible by selecting View in the menu bar. Click on SmartDimensions if it is not checked already.

Linear SmartDimension button.

2. A cylinder has two dimensions: radius and height. Add a height dimension to the model either by choosing Insert | SmartDimension | Linear from the menu bar or by clicking on the Linear SmartDimension button on the Technical Dimensions toolbar.

3. Move the mouse over the center of the cylinder's circular face until a green dot appears, indicating you have reached exact center. Click once to set the first point of the dimension.

4. Click on the Orbit Camera tool and rotate the cylinder until you are viewing the cylinder's opposite end. Then deselect the Orbit Camera.

5. Click on the bottom center of the cylinder to produce a height dimension on the model. If the dimension is left in the middle of the model, it will not be visible when the model is deselected. While the dimension is still yellow, move the cursor over the dimension value until a hand appears. Click and drag the dimension to either side of the model.

Placing a dimension along the length of a model using SmartDimensions.

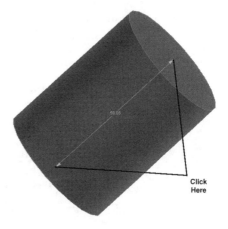

✓ **NOTE:** *If you wish to add text or tolerances to the dimensions, right-click on the dimension value and select Style Properties from the pop-up menu. The Style Properties dialog box provides the option of adding text before the dimension value (as a prefix) or after (as a postfix). Tolerancing can be set as upper and lower limits, or as a value with a plus and minus tolerance.*

Cylinder shown with prefix text with limit tolerances (left) and postfix text with plus and minus tolerances (right).

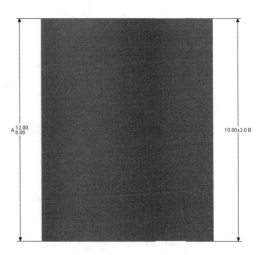

As mentioned earlier in this chapter, SmartDimensions are dynamically linked to models. To see how changes in dimension automatically reflect changes in geometry, complete the following exercise.

1. Select the Edit IntelliShapes button and right-click on the cylinder model. Choose Intelli-Shape Properties from the pop-up menu. Click on the Sizebox tab.

2. In an earlier exercise, you placed a dimension along the height of the model. Now, change the size of the model by entering a value of *12* in the Height field. Click on OK and view the updated model.

Updated model with height dimension.

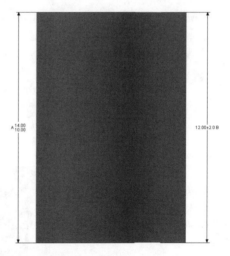

Creating Multiple Views

Only a few types of models, such as spheres or cubes, appear the same no matter which face is being viewed. When dealing with more complex shapes, the ability to use multiple views clarifies the nature of the models.

To create multiple views, right-click in a scene and choose either Horizontal Split or Vertical Split from the pop-up menu. Horizontal Split divides the scene with a horizontal line at the point where you clicked in the scene. Similarly, Vertical Split divides the scene with a vertical line. The dividing line can be dragged at any time to reposition it. To illustrate, complete the steps below.

1. Right-click in a blank portion of the scene and select Horizontal Split from the pop-up menu. Click on the border dividing the two views. Drag the border until the views are the same size.

Resize views by dragging the view border.

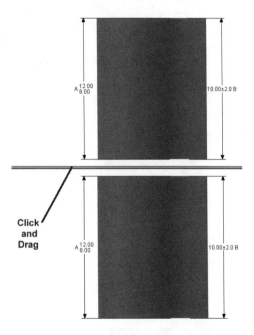

Radial SmartDimension button.

2. Use the Orbit Camera tool followed by the Look At tool to orient the top scene to view the top of the cylinder. Select Insert | SmartDimension | Radial, or click on the Radial SmartDimension button on the Technical Dimensions toolbar.

3. Click on the outer edge of the face to insert a dimension. As discussed earlier, you will probably have to move the dimension so that it is outside of the model. Click on the dimension and drag it to a new location.

4. Click in a blank part of the scene to deselect the model.

SmartDimensions will also change as you drag Sizebox handles to resize the model.

1. In the bottom view, click on the cylinder and drag one of the Sizebox handles until the radius dimension reads approximately 0.25.

Altered SmartDimensions displayed in two views.

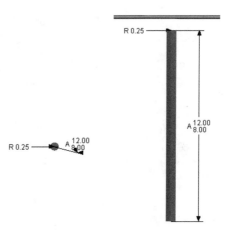

✓ **NOTE:** *By default, SmartDimensions associated with a model appear in all views. To turn off dimensions within a view, right-click in the scene and select Show from the pop-up menu. Toggle off the SmartDimensions box and click on OK.*

2. Right-click in a blank area of either view and select Remove View from the pop-up menu. Answer Yes to delete the camera used to create the scene.

3. Use the Orbit Camera to orient the scene so that both dimensions are visible and can be easily understood. Note that the values for SmartDimension remain readable as you rotate the scene. Save the wand in your catalog.

A single view showing dimensions in two planes.

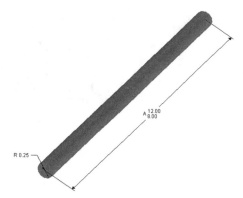

The use of multiple views can also be employed to simplify the arrangement of objects in 3D. A discussion of this issue appears in Chapter 7.

SmartDimensions can also be applied as driving dimensions, which can control the distance between shapes or models. Driving dimensions can be locked constraining the parent shape's movement to a fixed distance from the second attachment point. Smart-Dimensions applied between two separate models will always be driving dimensions. However, to apply driving dimensions to shapes within the same model, one of the shapes must first be selected as an IntelliShape or the Edit IntelliShapes button must be depressed. The shape selected first becomes the "parent" shape of the driving dimension. To edit a driving SmartDimension, click on the parent shape, right-click on the dimension value, and select Edit this SmartDimension. If the Edit options are grayed out, it means that the SmartDimension was applied as an annotation dimension.

Exporting a Model

The File | Export Model menu allows you to export 3D TriSpec-
tives models to other CAD programs. In turn, this permits the creation of detailed 2D drafting documents. The resulting models will
either be native to the application to which they are being exported
(*.3ds, .dxf, .obj, .wrl*), or become facet models (*.raw, .stl*). The following table lists the results of exporting selected TriSpectives
files to other 3D modeling programs.

Type of Model File	Extension	Result
3D Studio	3ds	Native to 3D Studio
AutoCAD DXF	dxf	Native to AutoCAD
Wavefront OBJ	obj	Native to Wavefront
Raw Triangles	raw	Facet
Stereolithography	stl	Facet
VRML 1.0	wrl	VRML file
POV-Ray 2.x	pov	POV-Ray2.x file

Using OLE

Embedding a Specification Sheet in a Scene

OLE (object linking and embedding) allows you to import data
from outside applications into a TriSpectives scene. For example,
a specification sheet created with a word processor can be embedded as an object into a TriSpectives scene. The following explanation and exercise illustrates this procedure.

Assume that you have created a new magic wand design and wish
to manufacture 10,000 units in time for the holiday buying season.
While you were creating an annotated model, your partner typed
up the manufacturing specifications using WordPad. Assume that
you wish to combine the specifications and annotated model into a
single file.

1. With the wand still in the scene, insert a new object by selecting Insert | Object.

2. The Insert Object dialog box allows you to choose between creating a new document and creating a document from an existing file. Click on the Create from File button, then navigate the *Inside* directory on the companion CD to locate the *Specs.doc* file.

3. Double-click on the *Specs.doc* file, then click on OK. The contents of the file are embedded as an object within TriSpectives. You can resize and reposition this object as you would other objects.

Specification sheet embedded in the scene.

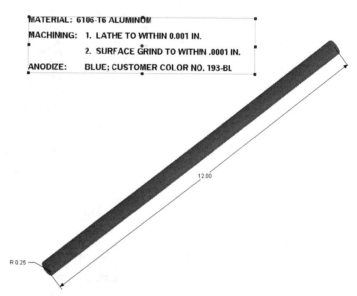

Embedding a Scene in Another Application

OLE can also be used to embed TriSpectives models in the body of documents in other applications, including word processing documents and spreadsheets. For instance, if you create a text document, you can illustrate the document by embedding a Tri-

Spectives model. To see how easy this is, try the following exercise using WordPad or another Windows 95 compatible text editor.

1. Open the text editor and select Insert | Object. Scroll through the Object Type list and select TriSpectives Scene if available. Click on OK. TriSpectives will start up within the document window, and will be fully functional.

A TriSpectives file embedded in a word processing document.

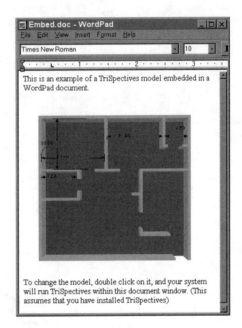

2. Drag a model from a catalog into the TriSpectives scene. Turn the model using the Orbit Camera tool.

✓ **NOTE:** *The host application will create a small window for your embedded model. This window can be resized within the host application, which will adjust the size of the picture accordingly.*

3. To close TriSpectives within the document, click outside of the window the host created for the model. The updated picture of the scene will replace the old one.

This type of object embedding can be used to send TriSpectives models to business partners or customers. If the recipients of the document have access to TriSpectives, they can edit the model and return it to you with comments.

Linking a Model to a Spreadsheet

You can also use other applications to control certain aspects of IntelliShapes such as length, width, or height. The following exercise will lead you through the process of linking a model to a Microsoft Excel spreadsheet.

1. Open a new scene by selecting File | New. Verify that the Edit IntelliShapes and Edit Surfaces buttons are not selected. Then drag a block from the Shapes catalog into the scene.

2. Right-click on the model and select Model Properties from the pop-up menu. Click on the Sizebox tab, and check the Show Formulas box.

3. To make the link to the Excel spreadsheet understandable to TriSpectives, you must enter an appropriate expression. Enter the expression *Cell[A1]* in the Length field. Click on OK.

4. Open Excel and arrange the windows so that TriSpectives and Excel can be viewed simultaneously. Drag the Block into the Excel spreadsheet. Enter a value of *5* in cell A1 of the spreadsheet. Note that the length of the block automatically updates.

TriSpectives file embedded in a spreadsheet.

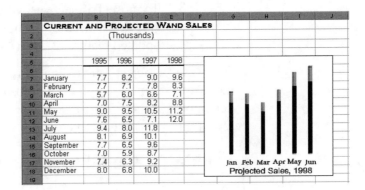

	A	B	C	D	E	F	G	H	I	J
1	**CURRENT AND PROJECTED WAND SALES**									
2			(Thousands)							
3										
4										
5		1995	1996	1997	1998					
6										
7	January	7.7	8.2	9.0	9.6					
8	February	7.7	7.1	7.8	8.3					
9	March	5.7	6.0	6.6	7.1					
10	April	7.0	7.5	8.2	8.8					
11	May	9.0	9.5	10.5	11.2					
12	June	7.6	6.5	7.1	12.0					
13	July	9.4	8.0	11.8						
14	August	8.1	6.9	10.1						
15	September	7.7	6.5	9.6						
16	October	7.0	5.9	8.7						
17	November	7.4	6.3	9.2						
18	December	8.0	6.8	10.0						
19										

7 Arranging Models in Virtual Space

This chapter focuses on arranging models to create intricate virtual scenes. Topics include using the TriBall tool and dragging techniques to move objects into and within a scene, employing multiple views to locate objects, and space planning.

Placing Models in a Scene

To illustrate the concept of placing models in a scene, models created in previous chapters and saved to a catalog will be used to make a stage and other items needed for a magic show in the following exercise. To begin creating the magic show, follow the steps below.

Open a new scene by selecting File | New. Verify that the Shapes catalog is open.

Create a Stage

To create a stage for the magic show, follow the steps below.

1. Select Format | Units from the menu bar and change the Length units to feet. With the Shapes catalog visible, drag a slab from the catalog into a new scene.

2. Click on the Edit IntelliShapes button, and then right-click on the slab. Select IntelliShape Properties from the pop-up menu and click on the Sizebox tab.

3. Enter a length of *15*, width of *20,* and height of *.25* for the dimensions of the slab. Click on OK.

Place Models on the Stage

1. Use the Look At and Fit Scene tools to orient the stage so that you are looking down on its top surface, as illustrated below.

Stage viewed from the top.

2. Unless the catalog you created earlier is open (*My Catalog*), access it by selecting Catalog | Open from the menu bar.

✓ **NOTE:** *If you did not save objects to a catalog earlier, open the* Inside *directory on the CD and select the* INSIDE *catalog.*

3. Ensure that the Edit IntelliShapes and Edit Surfaces and Edges buttons are not selected. Drag the table from the catalog and drop it near the bottom center of the stage. Note that the model landed upright on the stage because of its anchor location.

4. Use the Orbit tool to turn the scene so the table is located toward the front of the stage.

Table placed on stage by dragging and dropping.

5. Zoom in on the table using the Window Zoom tool.

6. Drag the Top Hat model from the *Inside* catalog and drop it on the center of the table. As illustrated below, the hat lands in the correct position due to anchor properties.

*Top hat correctly positioned
on table center.*

7.   Drag the wand from the catalog and drop it on the front right corner of the table.

Moving Objects Within the Scene

There are several ways to reposition objects once they are placed in a scene.

TriBall

Objects can be moved within scenes with tremendous ease using the TriBall tool, as illustrated in the exercises that follow. Begin by reorienting the scene.

1.   Select the Look At tool from the Camera toolbar and click on the front post of the table, as shown in the next illustration.

Click on the table post to reorient the scene.

Click
Here

Pan Camera button.

2. Use the Pan Camera to move the scene down until the hat is approximately in the middle of the screen.

3. Drag the Cards model from the *Inside* catalog. Drop the cards above the hat, ensuring that they do not land on the hat. Note that the cards will not be oriented properly; their position must be corrected. You could try to reorient the cards model using the 3D Shape Properties dialog box, but achieving precision through that method can be difficult. Instead, use the TriBall tool.

4. While the Cards model is still selected (indicated by the yellow outline), click the TriBall positioning tool on the Editing toolbar.

5. Move the mouse over the bottom handle of the TriBall until the cursor arrow changes to a hand icon. Click on the TriBall handle to make the selected axis the axis of rotation.

6. Place the mouse on the left side of the inside of the TriBall. Click and drag toward the right until the rotation value approaches 90 degrees.

Rotating the TriBall using the mouse.

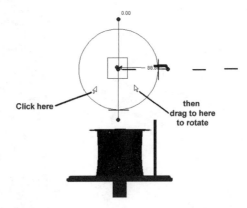

7. Right-click on the rotation value and select Edit Value. Enter an angle value of *90* degrees. Click OK.

8. Click on the right or left handle to select the horizontal axis as the rotation axis. Rotate the TriBall downward approximately 90 degrees. Grab the ball on the right handle and drag the cards model until it is centered above the hat, as illustrated below.

Cards model in final position above the top hat.

9. Deselect the TriBall by clicking the TriBall position-
    ing tool on the Editing toolbar.

Employing Multiple Views

When working in 3D, objects that appear correctly positioned from one perspective may, in fact, be placed incor-
rectly. By employing multiple views, you can determine the
true location of objects in 3D.

1. Right-click in the scene and select Vertical Split from
    the pop-up menu.

2. Move the scene divider so that the two resulting views
    are nearly the same size.

3. Use the Orbit Camera and Look At tools to orient one
    of the views so that you are looking down from above,
    as shown in the next illustration.

*Multiple views show the
true location of objects
in a 3D scene.*

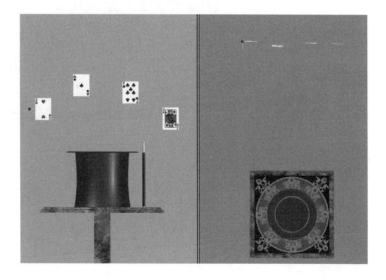

You can see that the cards are not directly over the top hat,
although they appeared to be in the first view. To position

them properly, take the following steps.

1. With the cards selected, click the TriBall on. Note that it appears in both scenes.

2. Use the squares on the TriBall to move within a plane. Move the cursor over the plane that appears flat in the top view. When the cursor turns to a four-way arrow, click on the plane and drag the cards until they are positioned over the top hat. Note that as you move the cards in one view they move in the other view as well.

The TriBall appears in both views, making 3D navigation easier.

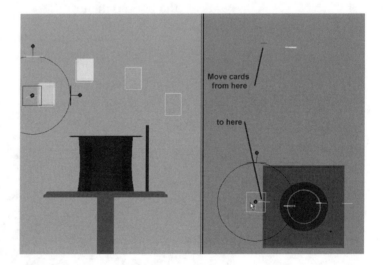

•➤ **TIP:** *All TriBall functions are active in all views simultaneously. For example, you can select a rotation axis using one view, and then move a model around that axis in the other view.*

3. Deselect the TriBall tool. To leave yourself with a single view, right-click in the front view and select Remove View from the pop-up menu. Enter Yes to delete the Camera.

Dragging Models within a Scene

Although using the TriBall is often the easiest way to move objects within a scene, it ignores all relationships established by anchors. As a result, you will not wish to use the TriBall when you drag an object along the surface of another object. Instead, you should drag the model, as explained in the steps below.

1. Click the Fit Scene button on the Camera toolbar. Select the *Inside* catalog tab, drag the birdcage object, and drop it to the left of the table.

2. Use the Orbit Camera tool to turn the scene until you are viewing it from the front.

3. Drag the still selected birdcage model to a desired location on the stage. The anchor maintains a perpendicular relationship to the stage, and the object slides along the surface. Move the birdcage model to a few locations on the stage to observe the flexibility of the dragging feature.

4. To save the scene, select File I Save As, input the file name *Stage*, and choose a directory. Click on Save.

Birdcage model dragged onto the stage.

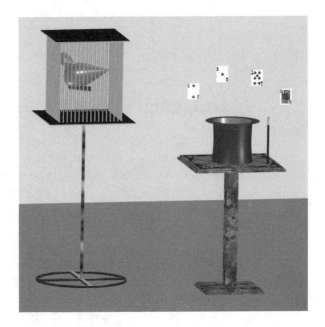

Space Planning

Space planning is especially easy using TriSpectives, as illustrated in the following exercise.

1. Select File | Open from the menu bar and navigate to the *Inside* directory on the CD.

2. Open the *Room.tmd* file. This file contains a 3D layout of a 900 sq ft home. Furniture is added randomly. Practice your moving skills by arranging the furniture.

3. Save the arranged house for use later.

✗ WARNING: *Due to the large number of surfaces in this scene, you should set Rendering to Wireframe before moving any of the objects. Doing so will greatly reduce the time required to move objects.*

Room.tmd features 3D
layout with randomly
arranged furniture.

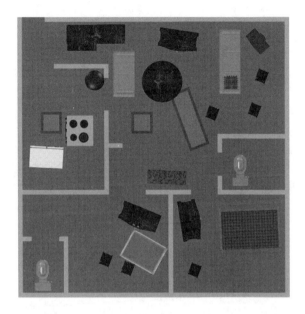

Same home layout with
one possible furniture
arrangement.

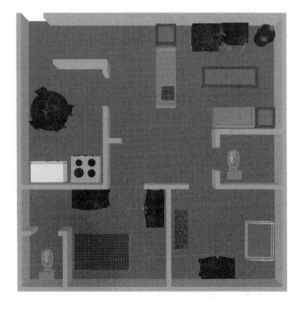

8 Enhancing Scenes

This chapter is focused on how to enhance the appearance of models and scenes created with TriSpectives. Topics include applying special effects to models, such as surface finishes, reflections, transparency, and emissions. Additional special effects that affect the entire scene include rendering level, ambient light, and adding fog. Exercises also encompass viewing a scene from new angles via the addition of cameras and customizing their positions, and adjusting perspective and exposure properties.

Object Effects

Finish

In TriSpectives, the term "surface finish" refers to the way in which a surface reflects and diffuses light. Surface finishes may be applied independently of appearance properties, such as color, texture, and bumps. There are two ways to apply a finish: by dragging and dropping it onto a model, or by using the SmartPaint Properties dialog box.

Adding a Finish Using Drag and Drop

The easiest way to add a finish to a model is to drag and drop a predefined finish from the Surfaces catalog. Complete the steps below to make an orange umbrella pole shiny and silver.

1. Open the *Picnic.tmd* file in the *Inside* directory from the companion CD. Verify that the Catalog Browser is visible. Open the Surfaces catalog by selecting Catalogs | Open.

2. Select the Edit Surfaces and Edges button from the 3D Shapes toolbar. Click on the umbrella pole, which is the surface you will be finishing. Click on Yes to regenerate the model.

3. Scroll through the Surfaces catalog to locate the Shiny Silver surface finish, then drag and drop it onto the umbrella pole.

The pole's color should have changed from orange to silver. If you missed the pole, and instead dropped the finish onto the background, employ the Edit | Undo function, and try again. If necessary, zoom in on the pole to make your target easier to view.

Adding a Finish Using SmartPaint

Finishes can also be applied via the SmartPaint Properties dialog box. Complete the exercise below to add a high gloss finish to a table section.

1. Right-click on the outer surface of the circular band around the legs of the table model, and answer Yes to regenerate the model.

2. Right-click on the surface again and select SmartPaint from the pop-up menu.

➥ **TIP:** *If Bevel Edges is the only option that appears when you right-click on the circular band, zoom in on the table* *model and repeat the right mouse click to access the pop-up menu.*

3. Once you are in the SmartPaint Properties dialog, select the Finish tab. The options on the Finish tab allow you to choose one of 12 predefined finishes, or use four parameters to set specific types of finish. Each option is explained below.

- *Diffuse intensity* controls overall light reflecting from objects.

- *Highlight intensity* controls the brightness of high-lights on an object.

- *Highlight spread* determines the size of the area affected by a light source's reflection.

- *Ambient intensity* controls the brightness of ambient illumination on the overall model and is affected by the scene's ambient light intensity (set in the Scene Properties dialog).

- Checking the *Metallic highlight* box gives the model a metallic look.

4. To give the object a high gloss, adjust the sliders as follows: Diffuse intensity, *100;* Highlight intensity, *100;* Highlight spread, *40;* Ambient intensity, *20.* Verify that the Metallic highlight box is toggled on.

✓ **NOTE:** *After you have adjusted the finish, you can view the results without having to exit the SmartPaint Properties dialog. Simply click on Apply. In addition, while setting a model's finish, you can check the Replace Surface Styles box to give the new settings precedence over settings which may have previously been applied.*

5. To create a mirror-like effect, click on the Reflection tab, and set the Reflection intensity to 90. Click on OK. Set the Rendering method to Realistic shading with the Ray tracing option, and render the scene by pressing <Ctrl>+R.

Try experimenting with other surface finishes in the scene using either the drag and drop method or the SmartPaint Properties dialog box.

Reflection

The Reflection tab in the SmartPaint Properties dialog box also allows you to adjust an off-scene image to reflect off of a model surface. Note that the reflection will not change the color of the surface. Change the rendering back to Smooth Shading with Textures and complete the steps below.

1. Right-click on the table top and select SmartPaint from the pop-up menu.

2. Click on the Reflection tab and select Reflect image. In the *Image* directory, double-click on the *Clouds.tif* file to select it.

3. Move the Reflection Intensity slider to 100 and click on OK. The reflected image appears on the surface of the table.

A cloudy blue sky reflecting off a glass table top.

You can use reflections to produce interesting effects. For example, you could create the reflection of a face in a surface without the need for a model of a person in the scene.

Transparency

You can make model surfaces partially or fully transparent. In the exercise below, you will turn the table top into glass.

1. Once again, right-click on the table top and select SmartPaint from the pop-up menu.

✓ **NOTE:** *To make an object completely transparent, all sides of an object must be selected. However, to simplify this exercise, the bottom surface transparency is already provided.*

2. Select the Transparency tab. Move the Transparency slider to *50.*

3. The way light bends as it goes through a surface is called refraction. You can change the refraction properties of any surface from the Transparency tab of the SmartPaint Properties dialog box. Slide the refraction index slider to *2.* Click on OK.

4. Verify that Rendering is set to display Realistic shading with Ray tracing, and then press <Ctrl>+R to render the scene.

✓ **NOTE:** *If Rendering is set to Facet or Smooth shading, a partially transparent object will be presented as if it were mesh. A completely transparent object will be totally clear. If you wish a transparent object to be realistically rendered, set Rendering to Realistic shading and Ray tracing. When fully rendered, colors or images applied to transparent objects will be visible.*

*Table with
transparent top.*

Emission

Emission creates the impression that light is being emitted from a model or surface, or that the model or surface is glowing. Emission also serves to brighten a model or surface, or to eliminate shadows.

Emission values can be set at 1 to 100; the higher the setting, the brighter the surface appears. Emission values affect only selected objects, and will not alter the appearance of other objects in a scene.

The appearance of objects with emissions applied is more obvious when the lights are not on, the ambient light is low, or the exposure of a camera is low. Emission is useful for making a window, TV, or computer monitor look like it is glowing in a dark room.

Scene Effects

Rendering

There are several ways to control how a scene is rendered, some of which have been covered previously. To view the Rendering options, right-click in a blank part of the scene and select Rendering from the pop-up menu.

The left side of the Rendering dialog box offers several levels of rendering. The settings range from (at the top of the dialog) the lowest quality image and quickest rendering time to (at the bottom) the best image quality and longest rendering time. While developing a scene, it often makes sense to employ one of the lower level rendering options as a time-saving method. After the scene is developed, the Realistic shading option, with its finer view but slower rendering time, becomes more appropriate. Rendering options are explained below.

- *Wireframe* rendering displays models as hollow forms whose surfaces are represented by lines.

- *Facet shading* displays an approximation of an object composed of a series of polygonal facets. Models appear as a solid color with shading.

- *Smooth shading* is more realistic looking than facet shading. Models appear smooth and are continuously shaded. Image textures will be rendered if the Show Textures option is checked.

- *Realistic shading* is the most realistic looking choice. With this method, lighting is more accurate and shadows are continuous and fine-grained. Rendering time is much longer; as mentioned previously, you may want to wait until a scene is nearly finished before selecting this option. Upon selecting Realistic shading, the following three options present themselves.

- Selecting *Shadows* will cause objects to cast shadows when light is shining on them.

- *Ray tracing* improves the quality of a scene's appearance by tracing the path of rays from light sources. Select this option to show reflections and refracted light.

- *Antialiasing* produces smooth, well-defined edges by interpolating the color of the pixels along a model's edges. This option also improves the quality of transparent objects and soft shadows.

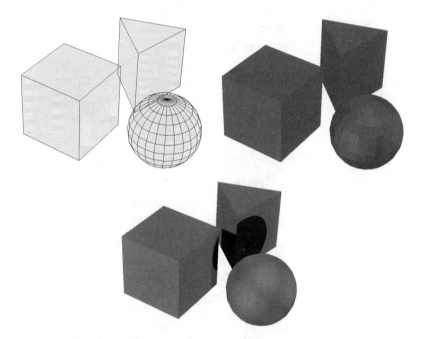

The same scene shown using three rendering options: Wireframe, Facet shading, and Smooth shading.

- Selecting the *Model edges* option produces colored lines on the edges of model faces and is used in combination with other rendering options. This option makes it easier to determine the exact positions of edges and faces. (This option does not appear when antialiasing is chosen.)

• *SmartRender* simplifies the style of model rendering during the editing phase only, thus saving you time because you will not have to wait for the scene to render after every change. Soon after you stop editing, the scene will automatically start rendering according to the level of rendering initially selected. If you do not wish to use this option, uncheck the Allow Simplification box.

Ambient Light

Adjusting the Ambient light level slider will alter the intensity of background lighting. Changing the ambient light will affect shadows and highlights. This type of light is not focused in any particular direction and is not dependent on the presence of light sources.

Fog

Adding fog to a scene creates a haze over objects. You can control both where the fog begins and the distance at which it is fully opaque. A gray fog has the most natural effect, but any color can be used. To give a background a foggy appearance, fog must be applied separately. Try adding fog to the studio scene with the following steps.

1. Set Rendering to Smooth shading or Realistic shading.

2. Right-click in a blank part of the scene and select Fog from the pop-up menu. In the dialog box, select Use Fog. Click on the Fit Distances to Scene button.

➥ **TIP:** *Even if you wish to manually set distances, using the Fit Distances to Scene button is a useful way to begin working. You can manually set the distances later.*

3. Choose light gray for the color of the fog. Click on OK and press <Ctrl>+R to render the scene. Once the scene has been fully rendered, it will look like a very foggy day at the beach.

Experiment with other colors of fog to discover the variety of effects you can achieve.

Camera Features

Recall that upon using the Orbit, Zoom, Pan, or other Camera tools, you are moving the camera rather than the objects in a scene. For instance, in Chapter 7 the split scene operation added a camera, allowing you to see each view from a different angle.

This section is focused on adding cameras to a scene and switching among them, and how to save a camera set to a specific view and reuse it. The latter feature is effective in presentations, for example, because you can quickly change the viewpoint from one angle to another. Finally, the section covers how to position cameras by clicking and dragging as well as through the use of the Camera tools.

Adding Cameras

To add a camera and gain a view from above the scene, take the following steps.

1. Select Insert | Camera, and then click in the scene. The umbrella and table from previous exercises should still be visible.

2. In the Camera Wizard dialog box, select Top and click on Next. Click on Yes to look through the camera, then click on Finish. Click on Yes to show all cameras.

The view may not be exactly what you expected. Use the Pan and Zoom Camera tools to reposition the camera.

Zoom Camera button.

Switching Among Cameras

To switch among cameras, select View | Scene Browser, and click on the plus symbol (+) next to Cameras. Note that two cameras are now focused on the scene.

Right-click on the first camera listed and select Look Through Camera from the pop-up menu. Click on Fit Scene to view the other camera.

Discerning which camera represents the top versus the front view can be confusing. To simplify matters, rename the cameras in the scene browser.

Click twice on the second camera in the list and replace its name with *Top View*. Press <Enter> to accept the new camera name.

Repeat the above procedure to change the name of the first camera to *Front View*.

Perspective tool.

> ✓ **NOTE:** *To verify the viewing direction of a camera, click on the camera within the scene. A yellow line will appear indicating the direction. A red dot also appears indicating the camera's "look at point," which indicates the area the camera is facing. If the Perspective tool is active, a gray cone will also appear indicating the camera's field of view. If you wish to verify the direction of a camera that is not currently active, click on the camera's name in the scene browser. The same set of indicators listed above will become visible.*

Positioning Cameras

Both the camera and the "look at point" can be positioned by clicking and dragging. They can also be positioned more precisely with the TriBall tool, the Camera Wizard, or the Camera Properties dialog box. The Camera Wizard can be used to determine a camera's distance from the scene and to choose predefined positions. The

Camera Properties dialog can be used to set the position and orientation of cameras using exact length, width, and height values.

Prior to changing camera position, several hidden models will be "unsuppressed." First, right-click on the *BackDrop* title in the Scene Browser and Select Model Properties from the pop-up menu. Deselect the Suppress box (bottom left corner) and click on OK. Repeat the previous procedure for the *Ground, Umbrella,* and *Camera & Tripod* models in the scene. If you cannot see all of the unsuppressed models, use the Zoom and Fit Scene tools to bring them into view.

Picnic scene with unsuppressed models.

✓ **NOTE:** *You may choose to unsuppress more than the prescribed set of models at this time. However, the greater the number of visible models, the longer each rendering will take.*

1. Now set the current camera's position so that it is representative of the camera model at the top of the tripod. Right-click on the Front View camera title in the Scene Browser and select Camera Properties from the pop-up menu.

2. In the Camera Properties dialog box, enter the Position, Look At Point, and Up Direction values shown in the next illustration. Do not click on OK yet because you first need to set the value of the view angle.

Camera Properties dialog box.

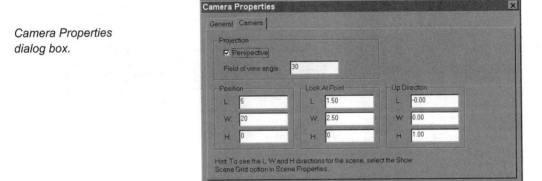

When the Perspective option is selected in the Camera Properties dialog box, the scene will appear to have depth. The amount of depth is determined by the Field of View Angle setting. When you use the Zoom and Fit Scene tools on the Camera toolbar, the Field of View Angle changes automatically. Other tools, such as Dolly, Walk, and Orbit, do not affect it.

3. Set the Field of View Angle to the value shown in the previous illustration and verify that the Perspective box is checked. Click on OK and then press <Ctrl>+R to render the scene.

Picnic scene as viewed through the tripod camera.

Camera Tools

Camera tools such as Fit Scene, Zoom, and Orbit have been introduced. The list below describes the functions of other useful camera tools.

- *Pan Camera.* Moves the camera sideways or up and down.

- *Dolly.* Moves the camera forward or backward in the scene, without altering the lens settings.

- *Walk.* Similar to Dolly forward and backward positioning, but also allows rotation.

- *Target Camera.* Moves the center of the scene to an object indicated by a mouse click. It also sets the rotation point for the Orbit Camera tool.

- *Save Camera* and *Restore Camera.* Allows you to save and restore preset views.

- *Perspective Camera.* Allows you to view a scene with or without perspective.

✓ **NOTE:** *Camera functions can be accessed via accelerator keys (F3, F4, and so on).*

Exposure

Exposure settings offer still more options for adjusting light behavior in a scene. To access the exposure settings, right-click in the scene. When the Scene Properties dialog box appears, select Exposure. Exposure settings are described below.

- The *Brightness* value affects the scene's overall exposure. Setting the value high makes the scene look overexposed, and setting it low makes the scene look underexposed.

- *Contrast* can be increased or decreased by moving the second slider.

- *Gamma* controls the appearance of shadows in the scene. Increasing the Gamma setting from default position brightens the shadow areas without changing the brightness in the rest of the scene. The Gamma setting cannot be decreased from the default position.

Click on OK to close the Scene Properties dialog box. Make the remaining models visible by right-clicking on each of them in the scene browser and deselecting the Suppress box on the Model Properties dialog box. Render the final scene.

Final scene.

Lighting and Shadow

This chapter focuses on altering the appearance and mood of a scene or object with lighting. Topics include lighting options such as intensity, color, and position; adding and removing lights and shadows from objects and scenes; the use of lighting types, including spot, directional, and point lights; and default lighting and other properties controlled through the Light Wizard and Light Properties dialog boxes.

Lighting

Whenever you open a new scene, white directional lights shine on the scene from four different directions. When you bring new objects into the scene, these default lights automatically reposition to accommodate the new objects. Test the default lights by taking the following steps.

1. Open a new scene and select View | Lights.

2. Click on Fit Scene to see the default lights. Moving the default lights and changing the direction of illumination are covered later in this chapter.

Default lighting for new
scenes consists of four di-
rectional lights.

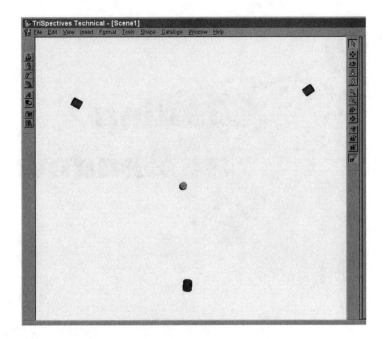

Adding and Changing Colors

You can change the color of existing lights in a scene, or the color of new lights as they are added. The process is similar to changing the color of any object. Follow the steps in the exercise below to change the color of a cube and the lights focused on it.

> ✓ **NOTE:** *Lighting effects will not be visible unless a scene contains an object.*

1. Drag a cube shape from the Shapes catalog into the scene. The default lights will adjust position when the cube is dropped into the scene.

*Default lights adjust to
accommodate new models.*

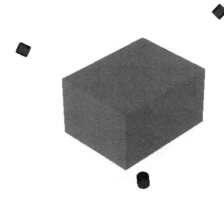

2. To change the color of the cube from the default color
(red) to white (thereby enhancing the effects of the
light change), right-click on the cube and select Smart-
Paint from the pop-up menu. Select White and click
on OK.

3. Click on Fit Scene. One of the four default lights may
be hidden from view behind the cube.

To add color to a default light, right-click on the upper right light,
and select Light Wizard from the pop-up menu. In the dialog box,
click on Choose Color and select a shade of blue. Click on OK,
and then click on Finish.

Note that the light has the strongest effect on surfaces it hits
directly, but little or no effect on surfaces facing away from the
light.

Combining Colors

The effects of using various colored lights can be seen by changing a second light to red. Use the Light Properties dialog to
change the color of another light.

1. Right-click on the left light and choose Light Properties from the pop-up menu.

2. In the Light tab, choose a shade of red. Click on OK.

Moving and Removing Lights

To move lights in a scene, simply drag them with the mouse. Click on the blue light now and drag it to several locations to see how the angle of the light affects the cube's appearance.

> ✓ **NOTE:** *Verify that the Edit Edges and Surfaces button is not selected.*

There are two ways to remove lights from a scene. First, right-click on the light in front of the cube. Click on Delete in the pop-up menu. The alternate method is to deselect Light On in the same pop-up menu by clicking on it. When a check mark next to Light On is absent, the light is present but off.

Adding and Adjusting Lights

Three types of lights may be added to scenes: spot, directional, and point lights. Brightness and a variety of other lighting features can also be controlled. Each type of light is represented by a different symbol within a scene, as illustrated below. Spotlights appear as cones. Directional lights appear as cylinders, and point lights appear as small spheres.

Directional, spot, and point lights (left to right).

Spotlights

Spotlights produce cones of light. You can control the brightness of a spotlight, the width of the area it will cover, and whether the spotlight edges are sharp or fade gradually. Add a spotlight to the scene by completing the steps below.

1.   Select Insert | Light. Position the cursor in front of and below the cube. Click once to open the Light dialog box.

2.   Select Spotlight from the dialog box. Click on OK and then on Finish.

3.   The gray cone is now visible. It indicates the area illuminated by the spotlight. Click on the light and position it to shine on the front corner of the cube. Then click anywhere in the scene to turn off the indicator cone.

✓ **NOTE 1:** *The TriBall tool can also be used to position a spotlight.*

✓ **NOTE 2:** *The effect of a spotlight is not seen until you select a realistic rendering level when the spotlight cone does not contain a vertex (the intersection of three surface edges).*

Cube with spotlight added.

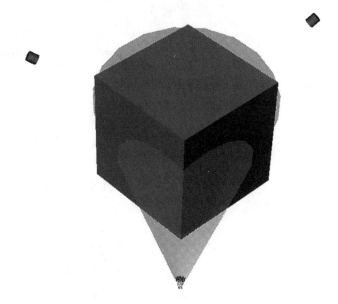

A more realistic sense of light can be created by working with the Rendering settings. This will, however, lengthen the time needed to render the scene. The next exercise illustrates this principle.

1. Right-click in the scene and select Rendering from the pop-up menu.

2. From the Style dialog box, select Realistic shading, Shadows, and Ray tracing. Click on OK.

3. Execute the Render Now command by pressing <Ctrl>+R, and then wait a bit.

You can also adjust the brightness of a spotlight and the area illuminated by its cone. Increase the brightness and narrow the cone area of the new spotlight with the following steps.

1. Right-click on the spotlight and open the Light Wizard dialog from the pop-up menu. Adjust the Brightness slider until it approaches 2.

2. Click on Next twice to go to the third page of the Light Wizard.

3. Adjust the Spotlight Beam Width to approximately *15*, and click on Finish. The cone will become much narrower.

4. Click anywhere in the scene to hide the indicator cone, and then render the scene by pressing <Ctrl>+R.

Spotlight after brightness is increased and area of cone light narrowed.

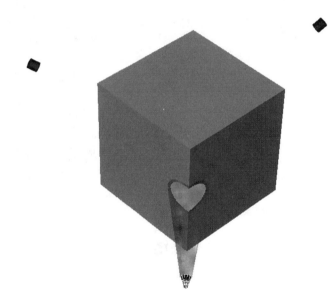

You can soften the effect of a spotlight with the *falloff* feature. This feature makes the intensity of the spotlight decrease toward the edges. To view the effects of falloff, complete the exercise below.

1. Right-click on the spotlight and open the Light Wizard dialog from the pop-up menu. Click on Next twice.

2. Move the Falloff Width slider to approximately *15*,
    and click on Finish. Note that the area covered by the
    gray cone now includes the actual spotlight area as
    well as the falloff area.

3. Click anywhere in the scene to hide the indicator cone,
    and render the scene by pressing <Ctrl>+R.

Spotlight softened with the
falloff feature.

✓ **NOTE:** *If the falloff width is set to a high number, the falloff*
may cover an area larger than the scene. When this occurs,
the gray cone indicator will appear as a circle around the
scene.

You can also set spotlights to cast shadows as discussed later in
this chapter.

Directional Lights

Directional lights illuminate the scene from a specific direction
and are suitable for simple lighting needs. By default, directional
lights are directed toward the center of the scene and automatically
adjust to accommodate the size of the scene. You can vary the

brightness and color of directional lights, and choose whether they will cast shadows.

As discussed earlier in this chapter, the angle of a light can be changed by clicking on the light and dragging it to the desired location. When you click on a directional light, the direction of illumination will be indicated by a visible line. As the directional light is dragged, it moves along the surface of an invisible sphere. If the light reaches the horizon of the sphere, TriSpectives will assume you want to move the light to the back side of the sphere. If you continue to drag the light, it will move behind the sphere. While the light is in front of the scene, the indicator light is yellow, and when behind the scene, it is red.

To adjust the brightness of a directional light, right-click on the red directional light in the scene and open the Light Wizard dialog from the pop-up menu. Move the Brightness slider until the value is close to 2, and then click on Finish.

The red light should appear brighter now. Click and drag the light to several locations to observe how the look of the cube is altered. Place the directional light next to the blue light. Note how the brighter light interacts with the dimmer one.

> ✓ **NOTE:** *If you add a new object while lights are visible, you may need to disable and then re-enable viewing the lights in order to see the final position of the directional lights. To do this, select View | Lights, and then select View | Lights again.*

Point Lights

A point light is similar to a ball of light. It shines in all directions. Point lights can be useful for modeling a lamp, making an object look like it is glowing, or illuminating the inside of a room. As with the other types of lights, you can alter a point light's brightness and color.

To see the full effect of a point light, make the cube into a hollow box as follows.

1. Select the Edit IntelliShapes button. Right-click on the cube, and then select IntelliShape Properties from the pop-up menu.

2. Click on the Shell tab. Check Shell This Shape and uncheck Start Section Open. Click on OK.

Now place a point light inside the cube by following the steps below.

1. Select Insert | Light. Position the mouse cursor above the cube and click.

2. Select Point Light from the pop-up menu, and click on OK.

3. Select Choose Color, and then click on a shade of green. Click on OK, and then on Finish.

4. Turn on the TriBall tool. Move the point light inside the box with the TriBall. You may need to turn the scene using the Orbit Camera to ensure that the light is inside the box.

5. Deselect the TriBall tool when you have finished. Turn off the other lights in the scene by right-clicking on each and deselecting Light On from the pop-up menu.

6. Click anywhere in the scene and then press <Ctrl>+R.

Box with point light added.

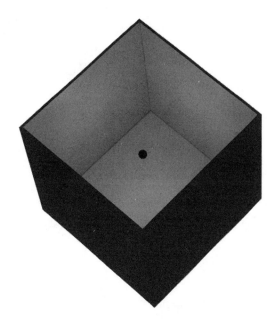

Shadows

In TriSpectives, all lights cast shadows by default. However, you can control the shadows from individual lights in three places:

- From the pop-up menu that appears when you right-click on a light
- From the second page of the Light Wizard as the answer to a yes/no question
- From the Light tab in the Light Properties dialog box

In the following exercise, you will turn shadows on and off to observe the resulting effects. First, you need to add another shape to the scene.

    1. Drag a slab shape out of the catalog and drop it near the bottom of the scene. Click on the slab to activate the Edit IntelliShapes mode.

2. Right-click on one of the handles and select Edit Size-box. Enter new values for the Length and Width fields that are approximately five times larger than the default values. Then click on OK.

3. Click on the model until the blue outline appears, indicating you are in Model Edit mode. Right-click on the slab and open the SmartPaint dialog from the pop-up menu.

4. Set the color to white and click on OK. Deselect the model by clicking in a blank area of the scene.

The finished slab should look similar to the one in the next illustration.

Slab added and resized to the same relative proportions as the cube.

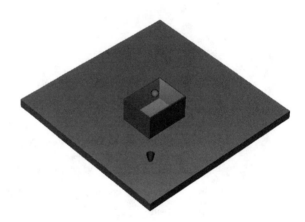

5. Now turn the red and blue lights back on by right-clicking on each light and selecting Light On from the pop-up menu.

6. Ensure that Rendering is set to Realistic Shading with Shadows. Press <Ctrl>+R.

The resulting scene should feature a red shadow to the left of the box and a blue shadow to the right. You will also note that the outer sides of the box are colored by the lights shining on them (the box is white), and that the stage is purple due to the combination of red and blue lights shining on the white slab.

Each light in a scene can be set to cast shadows or omit them.

Now see what happens to the scene when you prevent one of the lights from casting shadows.

1. Use the Fit Scene tool, if necessary, to make sure the lights are visible.

2. Right-click on the red light. Deselect Cast Shadows from the pop-up menu.

3. Click in a blank area of the scene to deselect the light and press <Ctrl>+R.

The formerly blue shadow is now purple, because the red light formerly blocked by the box has combined with the blue shadow. Note that the color of the objects has not changed, even though the color of the shadows has. The objects retained their color because turning off the ability to cast shadows prompts the light to act as though it penetrates objects.

Take a few minutes to turn shadows on and off for the different lights in your scene. Experiment with different combinations of light and shadow.

Additional Light Properties

The most common light properties can be accessed through the Light Wizard. You can create more complex lighting for spotlights, point lights, and directional lights using the options in their respective Light Properties dialog boxes.

Right-click on the spotlight and select Light Properties from the pop-up menu. The seven tabs in the Spot Light Properties dialog box are described below.

- The *General* tab contains information about the currently selected light, including its type and generic or customized name.

- The *Anchor* tab allows you to adjust the position of a light's anchor. This is similar to adjusting an object's anchor.

- The *Position* tab contains coordinates to set the position and orientation of lights in a scene.

- The *Light* tab controls lighting color, intensity, the ability to cast shadows, and the option to turn a light on or off. It also contains advanced shadow settings and additional options for controlling the beam of light in spotlights.

- The *Attenuation* tab contains options that control how far a light shines and how quickly the light diminishes near the edges.

- The *Gel* tab lets you project images onto objects similar to a slide projector. It also permits you to create a shadow of a selected image.

- The *Interaction* tab controls certain default behaviors of light in a scene.

Combining different lights and effects can produce visually rich scenes in a short amount of time. The image below is a good example.

Lighting effects can quickly add complexity to images.

This image is based on the scene created in this chapter. A simple backdrop was added on top of the slab. A gel was applied to the spotlight as a shadow mask. The spotlight's ability to cast shadows was turned off. The result is an intricately shaded scene.

Fitting Lights into a Scene

Let's return to the magic show. It is set to take place on stage and needs a variety of colored spot lights for theatrical effect.

1. Select File | Open. Choose the *Stage.tmd* file that you saved earlier, or the *Magic_show.tmd* from the *Inside* directory on the companion CD.

2. As mentioned earlier, all new scenes have four directional lights by default. To delete those lights, select View | Lights and click on Fit Scene. Then right-click on a light and select Delete from the pop-up menu. Repeat this step for the remaining three lights.

Before you begin inserting lights, verify that the Length units in your scene are set to feet. Select Format | Units from the menu bar. Then use either the Orbit Camera or the Look At tool to orient the scene so that you are looking at the front of the stage. Now place five new lights in the scene as shown in the next exercise.

1. Select Insert | Light. Place the first light above and to the left of the stage.

2. Select Spot Light from the pop-up menu and click on OK. Click on Choose Color in the Light Wizard and select Red.

3. Click on OK. Click on Next twice to go to the third page of the Wizard.

4. Set the width of the beam to *60* and the width of the falloff to *10*. You can do so by moving the sliders or typing the values directly into the appropriate boxes. Click on Finish.

5. Repeat the above steps four times to insert four more lights (green, yellow, purple, and blue). As you work, put each light to the right of the previous one.

It is possible to use the TriBall to position your lights. However, you can be more precise about light placement by using the Light Properties dialog box, as shown below.

1. Select View | Scene Browser from the menu bar. The scene browser makes it easy to access objects because it lists them in a tree structure format.

2. Double-click on Lights to access a drop-down list of the lights in the scene. The lights are numbered sequentially in the order in which they were added.

3. Right-click on the first light in the list. Select Light Properties from the pop-up menu. Then select the Position tab in the Light Properties dialog box.

4. Enter *16* for the location length, the distance from the center of the scene to the object, as measured along the length of the scene.

5. In the width box, enter *-12*, placing the object 12 feet to the left of center in the scene.

6. In the height box, enter *15* for the height of the light above the center of the scene. Click on OK.

Repeat the above steps for each of the remaining lights, with the following exceptions. For the second light, change the width value to *-8;* for the third light, change the width value to *0;* for the fourth light, change the width value to *8;* and for the fifth light, change the width value to *12.* When you are finished, the lights should be shining toward the center of the scene. If they are not, or if you would like to try different lighting angles, make adjustments using the TriBall.

Set Rendering to Realistic by right-clicking in the scene and selecting Rendering from the pop-up menu. Click on Realistic shading, Shadows, and Ray tracing.

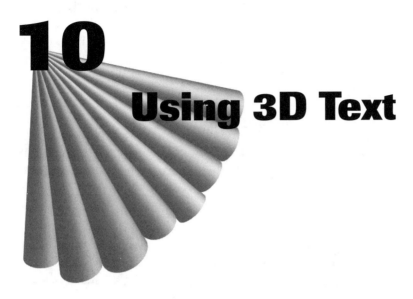

10 Using 3D Text

The use of 3D text can add tremendous impact to a scene. It can clarify or explain a picture, display a title or credit, or be used for dialog or subtitles in an animation. In TriSpectives, 3D text can either be added to a scene as a standalone object or blended into the surface of an object. You can vary the color, texture, and transparency of text in ways similar to such alterations of objects. You can also save text in a catalog for later use.

Adding Text to a Scene

The easiest way to add text to a scene is by inserting it. Take the following steps to experiment with scene insertions.

Insert Text Box button.

1. Open a new scene by selecting File | New. Select Insert | Text or click on the Insert Text Box tool on the 3D Shapes toolbar.

2. Click in the scene. When the Text Wizard appears, its dialog box will prompt you to choose settings for Size, Depth, Beveling, and Orientation. For the purposes of this example, accept the default options. Click on Finish.

3. When the text box appears, delete the word *Text* (the default) and insert *Magic Show*.

4. Click in the scene. The new 3D text will appear. You may need to rotate the scene or use the Fit Scene tool to get a clear view of the text.

Text Wizard makes inserting text easy.

Another way to add text to a scene is to drag it from a catalog. Catalog text objects have predefined sizes, fonts, bevels, and orientation. (If you choose catalog text that already has the features you want, you will have fewer settings to input.) You can also create text objects with your own preferences and save them to a catalog for use in other scenes. To do so, follow the steps below.

1. If the Catalog Browser is not already active, select View | Catalog Browser. Select Catalogs | Open and double-click on *Text.tsc*.

2. Drag the *5cm Upright* text object into the scene. Avoid dropping it onto the other text.

3. Replace the default text with your name, then click in a blank part of the scene to create the 3D text.

Scene with two text objects inserted.

Modifying Text

Text Wizard

Once you have placed text in a scene, you can use the Text Wizard to modify text features. Take the following steps to experiment with this process.

1. Right-click on the Magic Show text object and select Text Wizard from the pop-up menu. The first page of the Text Wizard prompts you to assign values for the text height and depth (thickness of the letters). Values can be typed directly into the fields or can be set using the scroll arrows next to the fields.

2. Enter *5* for the text height and *0.5* for the text depth.

✓ **NOTE:** *Changing text size may also reorient the text within the text box. Subsequent sections of this chapter cover adjusting text placement using the Sizebox.*

3. Click on Next. The second page of the Text Wizard provides beveling options for the text. Note that beveling will occur only on the text's front and back surfaces. Click on Flat for the edge type. Enter *0.1* for the distance the bevel will extend into the text.

✓ **NOTE:** *To work properly, the bevel depth must be less than or equal to half the text's depth or thickness.*

4. Click on Next to go to the third page of the Text Wizard. This page allows you to choose the way in which text will attach to objects. As you click on each option, the preview image on the left shows what the text will look like when it is attached.

5. By modifying the attachment method, you will change the orientation of the object in space. Set the orientation to Bottom, and then click on Finish. You may need to use the Fit Scene tool to view the modified text.

Text with modified orientation.

Editing Text

You can edit the contents of a text object. Follow the steps below to see this process at work.

1. Right-click on the Magic Show text. Select Edit Text from the pop-up menu. An editing box will appear. Change the text to read *The Fabulous Amazing Magic Show.*

2. Click in a blank area of the scene to display the new text. If necessary, use the Fit Scene tool to bring the text into full view.

3. The text will likely wrap, producing more than one line of text. You can restore the text to one line if you like by stretching the Sizebox until it is long enough to accommodate all the text.

Text before and after enlarging the Sizebox.

Drag Sizebox Handle

✓ **NOTE:** *Text Sizebox handles perform different functions than those of other objects. The horizontal handles control text wrapping; the vertical handles, text height; and forward and back handles, text depth.*

Text Format Toolbar

The Text Format toolbar allows you to change the font of a text object. The exercise below illustrates this process.

1. Select View | Toolbars and verify that Text Format is selected.

2. Click on the text until the Sizebox appears. The Text Format toolbar will also be activated.

➥ **TIP:** *When clicking on text, ensure that the cursor is over part of a letter. Otherwise, TriSpectives will make the scene active, rather than the text.*

3. TriSpectives uses the Windows fonts installed on your computer system. With the text selected, click on the down arrow that appears to the right of Arial. Select Copperplate Gothic, or another font you prefer.

4. Click in the scene to view the result of the changes. If necessary, stretch the Sizebox to fit the text on one line.

The Text Format toolbar can also control bevels. Three types of beveling—flat, round, and inverted round—can be used with any font, providing tremendous variety in text appearance. The following illustration shows examples of bevels and fonts.

Font and bevel samples.

Text Text

Text Text

TEXT Text

The Text Format toolbar also controls font size. Follow the steps below to create an appropriately sized sign for the magic show.

1. Click on the Magic Show text and set the font size to *24* instead of *12*.

2. Click anywhere in the blank scene to deselect the text. (Note that the text wraps again.)

Center alignment button.

3. Three different Text Format toolbar buttons are available to control the alignment of wrapped text. Set the alignment to Center by clicking on the appropriate button.

Finally, the Text Format toolbar controls italic and bold options for the text.

*Final formatting of the
magic show title.*

THE
FABULOUS
AMAZING
MAGIC SHOW

Text Properties Dialog Box

The Text Properties dialog box can also be used to control or modify text. It is very similar to the Model Properties and IntelliShape Properties dialog boxes discussed earlier in this book. The Text Properties dialog box contains information such as text object size, anchor location, and position of the object within a scene.

To explore the Text Properties dialog box, follow the steps below. You will be changing the thickness of the Magic Show text.

> **1.** Right-click on the text and open the Text Properties dialog from the pop-up menu.
>
> **2.** Click on the Sizebox tab. Enter a height of *10* in the Dimensions area. Click on OK.

The anchor location influences the way in which text objects attach to other objects in a scene, as well as the manner in which the text orients itself when used separately from another object. Complete the steps below to modify the Magic Show text.

> **1.** Right-click on the Magic Show text and select Text Properties from the pop-up menu.
>
> **2.** Click on the Anchor tab. Note that the anchor can be rotated around three axes, and that the angle of rotation can be set.

3. Set the L axis to *–1,* the W axis to *0,* and the H axis to *0.* Set the angle value to *90* and click on OK.

✓ **NOTE:** *As with other models, you can attach text to objects when the text is initially inserted. You can also change the text's anchor behavior to make it slide along a surface. To change the anchor, select the text, and then move the cursor over the anchor. Right-click on the anchor when it turns yellow. Select Slide Along Surfaces from the pop-up menu and drag the text over the surface of an object to attach it. Text shapes are facet shapes and cannot be used to create engravings on a model. In addition, they cannot be exported to SAT, STEP, or IGES files as part of an embossed model.*

You can reposition text in several ways. The most accurate way is to enter coordinates into the location fields on the Position tab of the Text Properties dialog box. The TriBall can also be used to accurately position text as discussed in Chapter 7.

Surface Properties

Colors, textures, images, bumps, and transparency can be applied to text to vary its appearance. You can isolate and work with the front, back, or side surfaces of individual letters by selecting the Edit Surfaces and Edges button on the 3D Shapes toolbar. If you want to work with all surfaces of a block of text, verify that the Edit Surfaces and Edges button is *not* selected.

Follow the steps below to enhance the appearance of the Magic Show sign.

1. Activate the Edit Surfaces and Edges tool on the 3D Shapes toolbar.

✓ **NOTE:** *If you edit the text, individual surface properties are removed. Adding individual surface properties as a final step is recommended.*

2. Zoom in on the Magic Show text and rotate the scene slightly using the Orbit Camera tool. Start at one end of the text and use the Pan Camera tool to move the text as you work. This will help you manipulate the surfaces of each letter more easily.

3. While holding the <Shift> key down, select several surfaces of different letters. After making your choices, right-click on the last surface selected. Select SmartPaint from the pop-up menu.

4. In the Color tab, select Image Texture, then click on Browse Files. Locate the *Images* directory and double-click on *Bluestr.tif* to select a texture.

5. Set Image Projection to Natural and click on OK.

TIP: *For best results when applying images to text, set the Image projection option on the color tab to automatic or natural.*

To experiment with different textures, select several other surfaces and repeat the steps above. Try the Dots, Overlap, Strings, and Splat textures using Automatic image projection; then try the Sine, Wave, Threads, and Lightbox texures using Natural image projection. When you have completed work on the surfaces, click on Fit Scene, and save it to *My Catalog*.

THE
FABULOUS
AMAZING
MAGIC SHOW

Magic show text with textures applied.

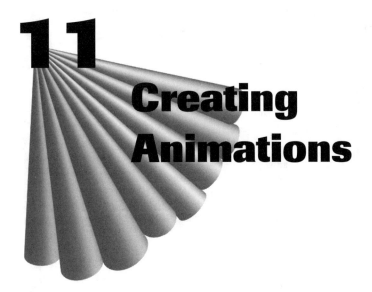

11 Creating Animations

This chapter focuses on animating TriSpectives models and creating animation sequences. These sequences can be used for applications such as exploded assemblies and fly-throughs, or as movie clips to illustrate assembly and disassembly. Topics in this chapter include motions contained in the Animation catalog; dragging and dropping predefined movements onto an object from a catalog; and using SmartMotions and the SmartMotion Editor for simple editing, timing within animations, and motion acceleration and deceleration. More complex editing will be covered in Chapter 12.

Animation Catalog

The Animation catalog contains predefined motions that can be added to a model for the purposes of animating it. Motions contained in the Animation catalog include Height Spin, Length Spin, Width Move, CorkScrew, Helix Down, Bounce in Place, and Fly Out. Also included are scale animations, which change the size of the model relative to the rest of the scene.

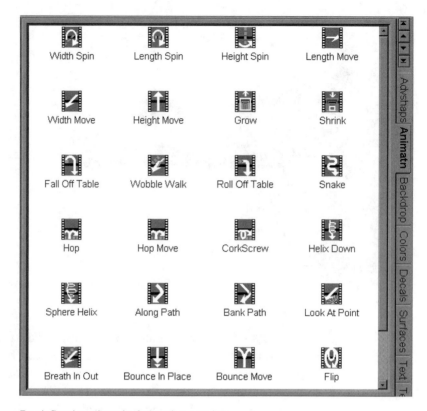

Predefined motions in Animation catalog.

SmartMotions

SmartMotions carry out simple animation editing functions, streamlining the editing process. The feature's intelligence saves you time and eliminates many tedious operations. For instance, if you change the end point of a path, SmartMotions will automatically adjust the path to accommodate the new end point.

To explore the workings of SmartMotions, take the following steps to add animation to the Magic Show created earlier.

1. Access the Magic Show by opening the file you saved earlier or selecting the *Magic.tmd* file from the *Inside* directory on the CD.

2. Use the Orbit Camera and Window Zoom tools to gain a clear view of the cards.

3. Click on one of the cards. Select Shape | Ungroup to remove the card grouping.

4. Unless the catalog browser is already visible, select View | Catalog Browser. Select Catalogs | Open and browse to locate the animation catalog file *Animatn.tsc*. Double-click to open the file.

5. Drag the Width Spin motion from the catalog and drop it directly onto the left card.

Animations can be stored in and retrieved from catalogs.

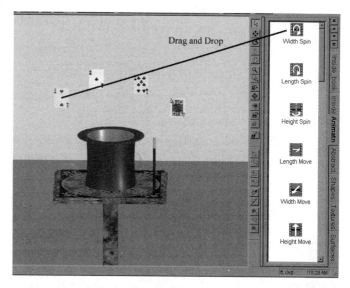

6. Make the Smart Motion toolbar visible by selecting View | Toolbars and toggling on SmartMotions. You have now created a simple animation and are ready to play it.

On button.

Play button.

✓ **NOTE:** *The SmartMotions toolbar must be activated to play animations.*

7.   Click the On button on the SmartMotions toolbar, and then click on the Play tool to play the animation. (Other playback options are discussed later in this chapter.) The card will spin around its width axis.

✓ **NOTE:** *Because a model spins around its anchor rather than its center, relocating or changing the orientation of an anchor will also change the behavior of the object's animations.*

Practice adding simple animation to two other objects in the scene by taking the steps below.

1.   Deselect the On tool on the SmartMotions toolbar. This allows you to add more animations to the cards.

2.   Drag a Length Spin motion onto the second card and a Height Spin motion onto the third card.

3.   Play the new animations by clicking the On button and selecting Play.

✓ **NOTE:** *You cannot add models or animations to the scene when the On button from the SmartMotions toolbar is depressed.*

Viewing Animations

Stop button.

Rewind button.

The function buttons on the SmartMotions toolbar include On, Play, Stop, and Rewind. Stop will halt the animation at any point during playback. Rewind sets the animation back to the beginning. As an animation is being played, the slider on the Timeline will move, indicating current location in the animation. You can also move the slider on the Timeline to see the position of models at any frame in the sequence. In addition, you may scroll slowly through the animation by clicking on the Timeline with the mouse and using the arrow keys to scroll.

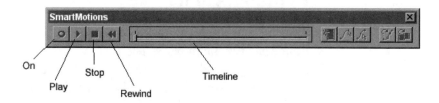

Use the SmartMotions toolbar when you want to view animations.

✓ **NOTE:** *The On button must be selected in order to scroll along the Timeline.*

The Key and Path tools at the right of the SmartMotions toolbar will be discussed in Chapter 12.

Combining Animation Sequences

Applying multiple animations is easy using drag and drop. When you apply more than one animation to a model, the result is a complex motion, as shown in the following exercise.

1. Drag a Length Spin and Height Spin motion onto the fourth card. (Verify that the On tool is not selected.)

2. Play the animation, watching how the fourth card has combined the motions of the second and third cards.

All motions in a catalog can be dragged and dropped onto objects. You can apply as many motions as you wish to each object.

✓ **NOTE:** *SmartMotions have fixed size values. If you create a small part, the SmartMotions in the catalog may cause the model to be off the screen for most of the clip.*

SmartMotion Editor

Refining Animations

The SmartMotion Editor can be used to refine animations. The Editor has two main parts. The first is a dialog box containing segment bars for each model and motion in the scene. The second is the Segment Properties dialog box, which allows precise editing of motion parameters. This dialog controls the timing of motions, the addition of timing effects such as acceleration, the ability to make motions repeat, and altering key points in the animation path.

To view the SmartMotion Editor, select View | SmartMotion Editor. Note that each model has a Track Group bar defining the groups. The bar controls the start time and total length of motions for the group. Any adjustments to the Track Group will result in similar changes to all underlying motions.

Double-click on one of the Track Group bars to expand it. When the animation sequences are in expanded mode, the topmost bar is the Track Group. Beneath the Track Group is the Model Source, which identifies the model affected by the motion segment. Beneath the Model Source are the model's motion bars. The length of the motion bars cannot exceed the length of the Track Group. A timeline showing frame numbers is located at the top of the SmartMotion Editor.

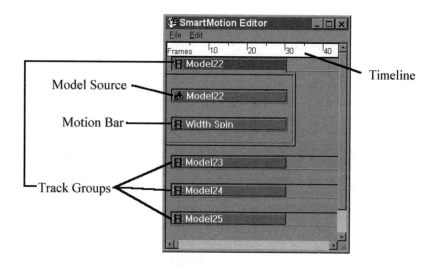

SmartMotion Editor graphical interface for adjusting the timing of animation sequences.

Animation Segment Timing

The length and timing of animation segments can be altered. For example, you may want the motion of one model to begin after the motion of another model ends. Take the following steps to experiment with these features.

1. If the SmartMotion Editor is not active, select View | SmartMotion Editor. Note that only models with associated animations are represented in the SmartMotion Editor.

2. Double-click on the Card1 Track Group to view the card model's motion bar. Alternately, you can view the motion bar by right-clicking on the Track Group and selecting Expand from the pop-up menu.

3. Verify that the On button on the SmartMotions toolbar is not depressed. Click on the Width Spin bar until it appears blue, and place the cursor at the *right* end of the bar so that the cursor becomes a double-ended arrow.

4. Click and drag the end of the bar to the left until the segment is half its original length. Double-click on the Card1 Track Group to condense it.

5. Double-click on the Card3 Track Group to expand it, and then click on the Height Spin bar. Drag the left end of the bar to the right until the segment is half its original length.

Dragging the end of a motion bar to adjust sequence length.

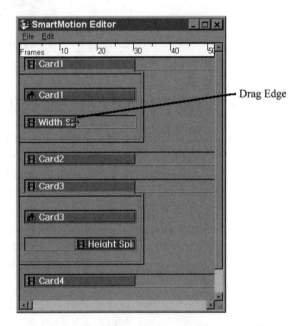

6. To view the effects of the changes, minimize the SmartMotion Editor and play the animation. Remember to select the On button before selecting Play.

✓ **NOTE:** *When you change the length of a motion sequence, the distance the model will move does not change. If the sequence time is shortened, the model moves faster to complete the motion path; if the time is lengthened, the model moves more slowly.*

The start time of a motion segment can be changed by simply dragging the segment within the SmartMotion Editor, as illustrated in the steps below.

1. The Card3 Track Group should already be expanded in the SmartMotion Editor. Expand the Card1 Track Group again by double-clicking on it.

2. Exchange the start times of the two segments by dragging the Card1 motion bar to the right and the Card3 motion bar to the left.

3. Drag the SmartMotion Editor until you can clearly see the models. You may have to adjust the size of the SmartMotion Editor window.

✓ **NOTE:** *You can play animations while the SmartMotion Editor is still visible. In fact, doing so will make it easier to view the results of your adjustments. As the animation plays, a vertical bar moves across the SmartMotion Editor, locating the animation's position in the sequence. You can also click and drag the vertical bar when animations are not playing to view the location of any models in the sequence. The vertical bar is present only when the On button of the SmartMotions toolbar is selected.*

4. Play the animation and observe the correlation between the motion segments' relative locations and the behavior of the models.

As mentioned earlier, changing the length of a track group will cause a similar change in the underlying motions within that group. To view this process, take the following steps.

1. Condense the Card1 and Card3 Track Groups by double-clicking on them.

2. Click on the Card4 Track Group in the Editor and drag the right end of the bar from 30 frames to 60.

3. Double-click on the Card4 Track Group and note that the Length Spin and Height Spin motions remained the same length as the Track Group.

Changing the length of a track group to alter the length of all motions within the group.

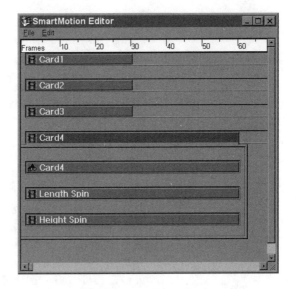

Timing can be set much more precisely using the Segment Properties dialog box. This dialog can be accessed by right-clicking on the Track Group bar, the Model Source bar, or the Motion bar. The contents of the dialog are determined by the specific bar selected.

Complete the steps below to set the lengths of all the animation segments to 2 seconds, and the start times to 0. You will be using the Segment Properties dialog box.

1. Condense and then right-click on the Card4 Track Group. Select Properties from the pop-up menu to open the Segment Properties dialog box.

2. Enter a value of *2* for the Length and click on OK.

3. Double-click on the Card1 Track Group to expand it again. Right-click on the Width Spin motion bar and select Properties from the pop-up menu.

4. Set the Track Start Time to *0* and the Length to *2* seconds. Click on OK.

5. Repeat steps 3 and 4 for Card3.

Because the motions in all Track Groups are now of equal length, you can precisely adjust the timing of the animation segments by once again using the Segment Properties dialog box. In the next exercise, however, Track Groups rather than motion bars are adjusted.

1. Double-click on the Card1 and Card3 Track Groups to condense them.

2. Right-click on the Card2 Track Group and select Properties from the pop-up menu.

3. Set the Track Start Time to *0.5* seconds. Click on OK. The segment bar will move to correspond to the new settings.

4. Repeat steps 2 and 3 for the remaining two Track Groups. Set the start times to *1.0* and *1.5* seconds, respectively.

5. Play the animation. The motions of the cards should start and end consecutively.

Acceleration

Motions can be made more realistic (or purposely unrealistic) by using the options found on the Time Effect tab of the Segment Properties dialog box. This tab is present only when editing a motion. Options exist for acceleration and deceleration, easing an object into or out of a motion, and creating a gravity-like acceleration within a motion. Follow the steps below.

1.   If the SmartMotion Editor is not active, select View | SmartMotion Editor.

2.   Expand the Card3 Track Group, right-click on the Height Spin bar, and select Properties from the pop-up menu.

3.   In the Time Effect tab, click on the down arrow for Type and select Ease In from the drop-down menu.

4.   Click on OK and play the animation.

When you select one of the Time Effect options, the dialog box may allow you to change time effect parameters, such as the strength of the effect. Experiment with the time effects and respective options before proceeding. Some of the effects may be easier to observe using motions other than spins.

Adding and Removing Motions

Motions can be added to existing Track Groups by dragging and dropping them directly into the SmartMotion Editor. The On button does not have to be deselected when you drag motions into the SmartMotion Editor. To add motions to the card animation, take the following steps.

1.   Condense the Card3 Track Group.

2. Drag a Grow motion from the Animation catalog and drop it onto the Card1 Track Group in the SmartMotion Editor.

3. Drag a Hop motion onto the Card2 Track Group.

4. Play the animation.

The effect of the grow is easy to recognize, but the hop is a little more difficult to see because it is combined with a spin motion.

Motions can also easily be removed with the SmartMotion Editor.

1. Expand the Card1 Track Group, right-click on the Grow motion bar, and select Clear from the pop-up menu.

2. Repeat step 1 for the Hop motion bar in the Card2 Track Group.

Exporting and Playing Animations

Animations can be viewed outside of TriSpectives by exporting them. An exported animation is a series of rendered frames which play back smoothly. When exporting animations, you can make the motions look smoother by increasing the number of frames per second. However, the number of frames that must be rendered while writing the file will also increase, thereby increasing the file size and the time required to save the file. The frame rate for animations is controlled within the Segment Properties dialog box. All motions within an animation sequence use the same frame rate.

1. In the SmartMotion Editor, right-click on an open area and select Properties from the pop-up menu.

2. Change the Frame Rate to *30* and click on OK.

Note that the frame number Timeline adjusts to accommodate the larger number of frames. In this case, when you play the animation, the distance that objects need to move between frames is reduced.

> ✓ **NOTE:** *When you change the frame rate, TriSpectives will use the new frame rate and the length (in seconds) of the animation to calculate the total number of frames required. When you play the animation within TriSpectives, it will play back at the maximum rate that your computer can render each frame, which is independent of the frame rate value. If you export the animation, however, the frame rate will be embedded, thereby retaining the correct animation playing time.*

As the animation plays, TriSpectives may simplify the rendering of the scene to increase the rate of playback. If you wish to fully render each frame, right-click in the scene, select Rendering, and uncheck Allow Simplification under the SmartRender option.

To advance slowly through an animation, ensure that the On button is depressed and click on the Timeline in the SmartMotions toolbar. Use the arrows to scroll one frame at a time. You can also start the animation at any point by clicking on any location in the Timeline and selecting Play.

More Elaborate Animations

When animations are added to groups of models, the entire group, rather than the individual models, will be animated. Animations that have been added to individual models will combine with the group animation.

In the next exercise, animations are applied to the cards to make them shuffle in midair and then return to the original location. Upon taking the steps below, remember to select and deselect the On button on the SmartMotions toolbar as needed.

1. With the <Shift> key depressed, select the third card and then the remaining cards in any order. The group anchor will be located near the center of the cards.

2. Select Shape | Group. Drag a Length Spin motion onto any one of the cards.

3. Go to the bottom of the SmartMotion Editor. You will see that a new Track Group has been added for the grouped cards. Right-click on the new group and select Properties from the pop-up menu.

4. Set the Length of the new Track Group to *3.5* seconds, and then click on OK.

5. Drag a Width Spin onto the Track Group and double-click to expand it. Note that the new animation sequence is the same length as the Track Group.

6. Play the animation to view the cards shuffling in space.

7. Save the magic show file with the new animations.

A magic show sign has been animated in order to illustrate the result of combining catalog motions. A Fly In motion causes the words to fly in and land over the stage. A Height Move causes the sign to move upward as the words come in. By staggering the timing, the words fly in individually. To view this sign, complete the steps below.

1. Click on Fit Scene to view the entire stage.

2. Drag the Sign model from the *Inside* catalog and center it about ten feet over the stage.

Sign model from the Inside catalog centered over the stage.

3. Play the animation. When you select the On button, the text will disappear because its position at the beginning of the sequence is outside the scene. When you deselect On, the text will reappear in its normal position.

The motions attached to the text will be automatically added to the SmartMotion Editor. Some animations such as Fly In are actually a combination of motions, and in the SmartMotion Editor they will appear as more than one animation bar. For example, Fly In has a Fly in and Grow bar and a Length Spin bar.

12 Creating Complex Animations

This chapter is focused on creating complex animations by developing new animation paths with the SmartMotion Wizard. Topics include using the SmartMotion Editor and the graphical animation path tool to edit key frames in animation sequences.

Key Frames

The key frame technique has often been used in traditional animation. The use of key frames traditionally allowed the artist involved in creating cartoons to lay out a series of important or "key" images. Later, those images were turned over to other artists, who would advance the process by creating the frames needed between the key frames. This technique was a tremendous time saver for the original artist.

TriSpectives mimics the key frame technique by allowing you to set the position and orientation of objects at key frames. TriSpectives then fills in the areas between the frames for you.

Customizing Paths

Creating a Custom Path

Chapter 11 covered how to drag and drop animation sequences onto objects. There will be times, however, when your needs cannot be met by animations from the catalog, and it will be necessary to develop custom paths. In the next exercise, a general path is created for an object using the SmartMotion Wizard. You will produce a path for a toy truck designed to drive along a road.

Add New Path tool.

1. Access the *Inside* directory of the companion CD and open the *Drive.tmd* file.

2. Select the truck by clicking on it. Then click on the Add New Path tool on the SmartMotions toolbar.

3. The SmartMotion Wizard will appear and present you with the option of creating a spin, move (along a single direction), or custom path. Select Custom and click on Next.

4. Set the motion length to *15* seconds.

5. Click on Finish. A grid should now be visible beneath the truck. You will create the path of this object and edit it directly on the grid, providing visual feedback as key frames are created.

Animation grid.

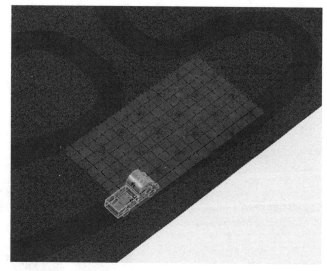

*Extend Path
button.*

6. Click the Extend Path tool on the SmartMotions toolbar. Then click on the road in front of the truck to form
a path for the truck.

*Extending the anima-
tion path.*

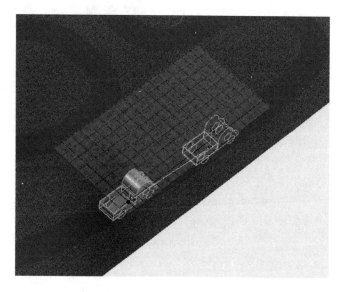

The animation now contains two key frames. The first is the start point, and the second is the end point. As you continue to extend the path, each successive key frame is added to the end of the animation sequence. Note that only the beginning and end frames remain highlighted, while the key frames in between are marked with an orientation marker, as shown in the following illustration.

Key frames represented by orientation markers.

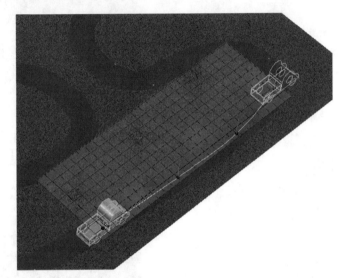

7. Add several more frames along the road. When you are finished, deselect the Extend Path tool.

8. Click the On button and then Play to see the truck follow the custom path.

Changing Path Orientation

As you add key frames to the animation, you will notice that the truck consistently faces the same direction by default. To change the direction of the model in the animation, complete the steps below.

1. Deselect the On button. Click on the truck, and then right-click on the motion path.

2. Select Animation Path Properties from the pop-up menu.

3. Set the Orient At Type to Along Path. Click on OK, and then play the animation. The truck will now face the direction of the path as it moves.

When you create a custom animation, the orientation of an object during the sequence is determined by its orientation in the first key frame. At each key frame, the orientation marker shows the Orient Up direction in green and the Orient At direction in blue. To view the orientation markers, deselect the On button, click on the truck, and then click on the line with the left mouse button.

An important advantage of editing on-screen is the ability to drag key frame markers to new locations. This simplifies the process of visualizing changes as you work.

1. Click on the second key frame marker. When you click on a key frame marker, a wireframe image of the model will appear, showing you the orientation of the model at that point.

2. Now drag the marker perpendicular to the path. As you click and drag the key frame marker around, note that the orientation of the model changes to point along the path. If you look carefully, you can also see the blue indicator at the first key frame pointing along the new path.

3. To ensure that the truck's path does not leave the road, return the key frame marker to its original position.

When you play the animation, the path and orientation of the object will be interpolated between the key frames. The interpolation method can be set to Spline, which will create smooth transitions along the path, or Linear, which will cause abrupt changes at key frames. To see the difference between these two interpolation options, take the following steps.

1. Right-click on the motion line and select Animation Path Properties from the pop-up menu.

2. Change the Interpolation Type to Linear and click on OK. The path line between the key frames is now straight.

3. Change the Interpolation Type back to Spline.

Extending the Path

Next, you must add enough key frames so the truck can navigate all the way around the road. Complete the steps below to add more key frames.

1. To ensure that the animation path is visible, verify that the On button on the SmartMotions toolbar is not depressed. Then click on the truck.

2. Click on the path to access the animation grid. Select the Extend Path tool on the SmartMotions toolbar and click along the road to add key frames. The frames should be spaced about two truck lengths apart, but for now do not insist on precision.

3. Continue to add key frames until you have almost reached the first key frame. Then deselect the Extend Path tool.

The Extend Path tool can be used to add key frames.

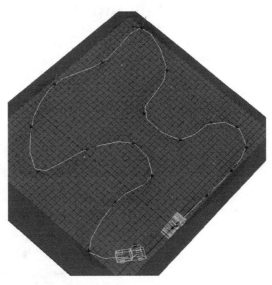

4. Right-click on the path and select Animation Path Properties from the pop-up menu. Click on Close Path, then click on OK.

A key frame has been added at the end of the path to bring the truck back to its starting place.

Using the Close Path option will ensure that animations look smooth when played in a continuous loop.

Adding Intermediate Frames

If you have inserted too few points on the animation path, the truck will probably drive off the road from time to time. The next exercise illustrates how to correct this situation. The Insert Key tool is used to add intermediate key frames at points along the path.

Key frames can be inserted at any point along an existing animation path using the Insert Key tool.

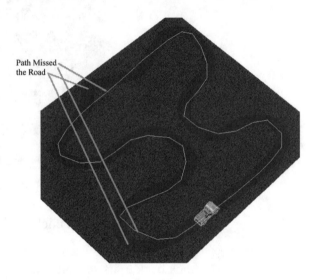

1. Unless the path and animation grids are visible, click on the truck and then on the path to turn them on.

Insert Key tool.

2. Select the Insert Key tool on the SmartMotions toolbar. The cursor will appear as cross hairs.

3. When you locate a portion of the path that goes off the road, click on the path (not on the road) between the relevant key frames. A new key frame appears at the point.

4. Adjust the position of the new key frame marker to better align the path with the road.

5. Continue to add key frames as needed by repeating steps 2 through 4.

6. Play the animation by clicking the On button and then on Play.

Animating the Third Dimension

Adding Height to a Key Frame

Editing on-screen also makes it easier for an object to follow a three-dimensional path. Complete the following exercise to make the truck drive over an obstacle.

1. Make the animation grid visible, if it is not already.

2. Drag the Pog Stack from the Inside catalog and drop it at the second key frame point in the truck's path, as illustrated below.

Drop the Pog Stack on the key frame marker.

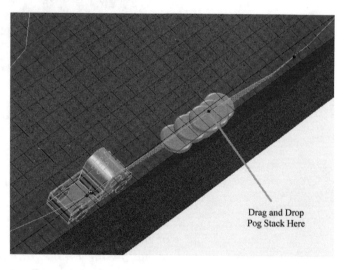

Drag and Drop
Pog Stack Here

3. When you drop the Pog Stack, the animation grid and path disappear. Make the animation grid visible again by clicking on the truck and then on the path.

4. Click on the key frame marker at the point at which the Pog Stack has just been dropped. A wireframe of the truck will appear. Search the marker closely (you may need to zoom in) to find a small square at the top. This square is the elevation handle.

5. Click and drag the elevation handle upward so the truck goes over the Pog Stack.

Drag the elevation handle to give the path a third dimension. TriSpectives fills in the area between the animation grid and path.

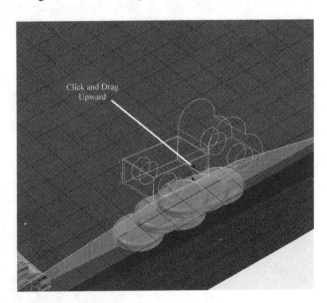

6. Play the animation.

•❖ **TIP:** *To make the animation appear smoother during play-back, increase the number of frames per second by opening the SmartMotion Editor, right-clicking on a blank part of the Editor, and selecting Properties from the pop-up menu. Set the Frame Rate to 30 instead of 15 frames per second and click on OK to close the Segment Properties dialog box.*

Positioning Models in Key Frames with the TriBall

A simple way to add special animation effects is to use the TriBall to position models at key frames. In the following exercise, realism is added to the movement of the truck by giving it "roll" while it takes tight turns.

1. Ensure that the On button is deselected and click on the truck.

2. Click on the path to display the animation grid. Then click on the anchor of the key frame positioned at the first turn.

3. Select the TriBall tool from the Editing toolbar. Rotate the TriBall to turn the truck up on two wheels, leaning to the outside of the turn. At this point, you can use the TriBall to place the truck in any position or orientation you desire.

4. From the SmartMotions toolbar, select the Next Key in Path button.

5. Repeat steps 3 and 4 for the remaining turns, placing as much roll on the model as you wish. Play the animation.

Next Key in Path button.

A sample animation of the truck traveling the road is available in the *Truck.tmd* file in the *Inside* directory of the companion CD.

Complex Motion in 3D

As discussed in Chapter 11, more than one animation path can be added to a model. The resulting animation is a blending of the paths. An alternative method is to use the Key Frame Properties dialog box to edit position and orientation properties at key frames. Both methods have merit, and the decision of which to use will depend on preference, experience, and the interdependence of the two animation sequences. For instance, if you animate a human figure so that it appears to dance (using different dance moves), you might place another animation parallel to the first. The second animation could appear to move around the room. The combination of the two animations would give the figure the appearance of dancing around the room. In this case, the benefit of having two animations is that the path the figure takes around the room can be altered without changing the dance move animation.

Creating a Fly-through

Creating a fly-through in TriSpectives is accomplished by adding motions to a camera. Once you have added the motions, you can save the animated camera to a catalog for future use. In this section, the SmartMotion Editor and graphical animation tools are used to create a fly-through tour of the house arranged in Chapter 7.

Set Up the Scene

First, set up a scene for the fly-through.

1. Turn off the Catalog Browser to create more space on the screen. Open the arranged house file saved in Chapter 7, or the *House.tmd* file from the *Inside* directory on the companion CD.

2. Use the Look At and Orbit Camera tools to arrange the scene so that you are viewing from above the house; the door will appear at the top of the scene.

3. Select Insert | Camera, and then click in the scene to place the camera.

4. Select Back when you are prompted to insert the direction of the camera and enter *8* (feet) when asked "how far away the camera should be."

5. Click on Finish, and then click on Yes to show the cameras. Use the TriBall to move the camera. Move the mouse cursor over the TriBall so that a four-way arrow appears, and then drag the camera just outside the door of the house pointing into the kitchen.

TriBall being used to move the camera.

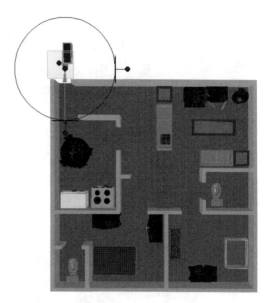

Next, split the scene to make creating a fly-through easier. One half of the scene can be used to view the path of the camera, while the other half can show the scene through the camera at each key frame. The split-screen method also provides more flexibility in camera positioning. Continue setting up the scene and camera by completing the following exercise.

1. First, split the scene by right-clicking in a blank area of the scene and selecting Vertical Split from the pop-up menu. Then adjust the vertical divider line to make the size of each view approximately the same.

2. In the right view, right-click on the camera and select Look Through Camera from the pop-up menu.

3. To reduce rendering time, set Rendering in the left view to Wireframe, and in the right view to Facet.

4. Using the Pan Camera tool, position the scene in the right view so that the camera looks through the doorway. Then deselect the tool.

5. In the left scene, right-click on the camera and select Camera Properties from the pop-up menu.

6. Verify that the Perspective option is checked in the Projection field, and then set the Field of view angle to *60.*

7. In the Look At Point field, set the height (H) value to *5* (feet), the average eye height. Click on OK.

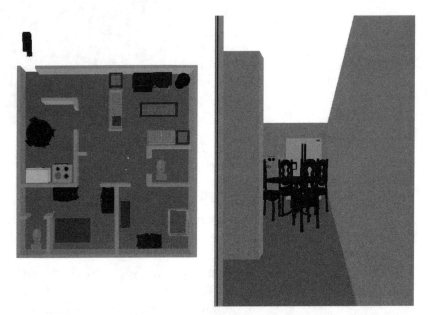

Use a split scene to simultaneously view the camera path and view through the camera.

Create a Path

To create the animation pathway, take the following steps.

1. In the left view, click on the camera and then select the Add New Path tool on the SmartMotions toolbar.

2. Select Custom Motion on the SmartMotion Wizard, and then click on Next. Enter *10* for the length of the motion and click on Finish.

3. Select the Extend Path tool. Then create a path for the camera to travel on by clicking on locations for key frames. Use the following key frame positions.

   Key point 2: Just inside the kitchen door near the table.

   Key point 3: In the doorway between the kitchen and the living room.

   Key point 4: In the living room, behind and near the left end of the couch.

   Key point 5: In the hall, near the master bedroom door.

   Key point 6: On the right side of the master bedroom.

   Key point 7: In the master bedroom just to the left of the previous point.

4. Deselect the Extend Path tool.

Seven key frames for the house fly-through.

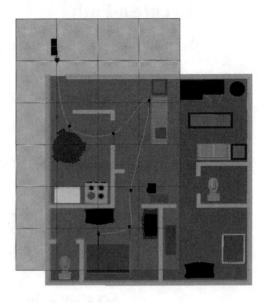

5. Play the animation by clicking On and then Play on the Animation toolbar.

Orient the Camera

Like the truck path mentioned earlier in the chapter, the camera has consistently faced the same direction throughout the animation because of its default setting. In the exercise below, the direction of the camera is edited to make the fly-through more realistic.

1. Deselect the On button. Click on the camera, and then on the motion line.

2. Right-click on the third key frame anchor (in the doorway between the kitchen and living room), and then select Key Frame Properties from the pop-up menu.

3. Go to the Position tab and enter a value of *-45* when prompted to set the rotation angle of the camera pan. Click on OK. Note that the wireframe representation of the camera at this key frame has now rotated toward the living room.

4. Right-click on the next key frame anchor and repeat steps 2 and 3, changing the Pan angle to *-90*. Click on OK.

✓ **NOTE:** *To avoid losing the camera's animation, do not delete the camera when leaving split screen mode.*

The steps below use the TriBall to adjust the Pan angle of the fifth and seventh key frames.

1. Click on the fifth key frame anchor with the left mouse button and select the TriBall tool from the Editing toolbar.

2. To change only the Pan angle of the camera, place your cursor on the outline of the TriBall until it appears as a rotation arrow.

3. Rotate the TriBall counterclockwise until the camera is facing the dresser on the right side of the bedroom. Deselect the TriBall tool.

4. Repeat steps 1 through 3 for the seventh key frame, rotating the camera until it faces the left wall of the bedroom.

5. Play the animation. Save the animated house file for use later in this chapter. Name the file *House_anim.tmd*.

✓ **NOTE:** *Be consistent when choosing the Pan angle. For example, if one key point has a pan of 350° and the next has a pan of -10°, the camera will make a 360° turn between these two key points.*

Using Animation to Explode an Assembly

Animations are useful in creating exploded views, which illustrate each individual part of a complex assembly. A useful feature of animations in this context is their ability to explode an assembly without changing the position of the original model. To view an example, open the *Explode.tmd* file in the *Inside* directory of the companion CD and play the animation. If you would like to study the motions added to the models and the timing of those motions, use the SmartMotion Editor.

Exploded view of a piston and crank-shaft assembly.

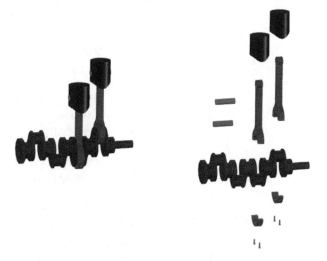

Animations can also be used to create training videos on the assembly and disassembly of objects. An example of a simple training video can be found in the*Training.tmd* file on the companion CD.

Articulating Assemblies

As mentioned earlier, with the use of animations, you can control the position and rotation of models in all three planes, as well as the timing and rate of motions. By combining motions on various models, an articulated assembly can be simulated.

> ✓ **NOTE:** *TriSpectives Technical does not have the capability to create true kinematic motions.*

When you animate several objects in the same scene, it helps to label each object before you start work. When adding an animation to an object, the name given to it will appear on the Track Group bar in the SmartMotion Editor. In this section, an articulated assembly animation is created for the partial engine model you observed in the exploded view. Each of the objects has already been labeled.

To begin, open the *Piston.tmd* file in the *Inside* directory of the companion CD. Drag a Length Spin motion from the Animation catalog onto the crankshaft.

The bottom of the connecting rod should travel in a circle, while the top (with the piston) must travel straight up and down. The anchor of the rod has been placed at the center of the top hole to simplify the motion simulation. In the following exercise, a new animation is placed on the first connecting rod.

1. Open the Scene Browser by selecting View | Scene Browser. The names of the models in the scene should be visible.

2. Click on the (+) symbol in front of the *Piston1_Assy* model to expand the group. The group contains a piston, rod, and pin.

3. Select the *Rod1* model by clicking on the model in the Scene Browser. Add a new animation path to this model by selecting Add New Path from the SmartMotions toolbar.

4. In the SmartMotion Wizard, select Spin and enter a value of zero for the number of degrees to spin by. Click on Next.

5. Accept the default length of the animation by clicking on Finish.

Next, the SmartMotion Editor is used to add seven additional key frames to the new animation to make a total of nine frames. The completed animation will make the rod swing like a pendulum. (Entering the value of zero in step 4 above is what will allow the pendulum to return to the center.) Later, when the swinging motion is combined with an up and down motion, the base of the rod will appear to follow the circular path of the crankshaft. Continue by taking the following steps.

1. Open the SmartMotion Editor and double-click on the Rod1 track group to expand it. Right-click on the Length Spin bar, and then select Properties from the pop-up menu.

2. Click on the Path tab, and note that it contains two keys. The first key is the current one. Additional frames are added behind the current frame. You cannot add key frames after the last one in the sequence.

3. Click on the Insert Key button. Note that the number of keys has been raised to three, and that the key you just added has become the current key.

4. Continue to click the Insert Key button until the total number of keys reaches nine.

Path tab in Segment
Properties dialog.

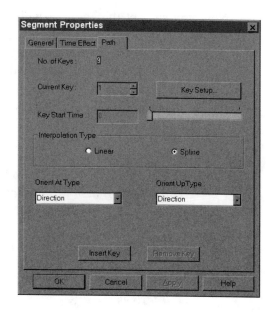

Before you set the positions in each of the key frames, it is important to set each Key Start Time. When a new key frame is added to an existing animation, it is centered halfway between the two frames before and after. In the previous exercise, each of the new key frames was added between the last and next to last frames, reducing the time allotted for each frame by half. If you scroll through the key frames by clicking the up and down arrows next to the Current Key value, you will see that the first key frame is at 0, the next at 0.5, the third at 0.75, and so on.

✓ **NOTE:** *Key start times always range from zero to one in value, regardless of the length of the animation in seconds.*

Set the values of the Key Start Times to the values shown below by first selecting each frame with the Current Key arrows, and then moving the Start Time slider.

Key frame	1	2	3	4	5	6	7	8	9
Key Start Time	0	.12	.25	.37	.5	.62	.75	.87	1

Now you can set the angle at which the rod will roll for each of the key frames. The angular orientation of each key frame employs a unique terminology. Imagine that you are the pilot of an airplane: tilt refers to the amount that the nose is raised or lowered, and corresponds to rotation around the width axis. Roll refers to the side to side angle of the wing with the ground relating to rotation around the length axis. Pan would be the motion created by the rudder, turning the plane around the height axis.

> ✓ **NOTE:** *The direction of an object's axis, and not the global coordinate system of the scene, will determine the relative position for that object.*

Complete the steps below to set the roll angle for the rod.

1. Set the Current Key to *2* by clicking on the up or down arrows.

2. Click on the Key Setup button, and then click on the down arrow at the right of the Key Parameter box.

3. Select Roll and then enter a value of *-7* (degrees). Click on OK.

4. Click on the up arrow at the right of the Current Key value to go to the next key frame.

5. Repeat steps 2 through 4, entering the values below for each of the key frames. Since frames 5 and 9 will have values of zero, there is no need to edit their key properties.

Key frame	3	4	6	7	8
Roll	-11	-7	7	11	7

> ✓ **NOTE:** *When you animate grouped shapes and then ungroup them, you will lose the animation because the "group" no longer exists.*

6. Play the animation and note that the rod swings at the same rate at which the crankshaft rotates.

Now, add motions to the group containing the rod, piston, and pin by taking the steps below.

1. Select the *piston1_Assy* model from the Scene Browser.

2. Drag and drop two Height Moves from the Animation catalog onto the piston model. Verify that the Smart-Motion Editor is open. Double-click on the *piston1_Assy* track group to expand it.

The piston movement should be slowed at both the top and bottom of the stroke. This can be accomplished, in part, by using a time effect called EaseBoth, which affects the beginning and end of a motion. To regulate the piston movement, an EaseBoth must be applied to one Height Move for the down stroke and another height move for the up stroke. Take the following steps to set the time effect for each of the Height Moves.

1. Right-click on the first Height Move motion bar and select Properties from the pop-up menu.

2. Select the Time Effect tab and set the Type to Ease-Both.

3. Adjust the strength of the acceleration to *0.6* by moving the slider.

4. Repeat steps 1 through 3 for the second Height Move.

Because the total time of the engine animation is two seconds, each of the piston motions (up and down) should last one second. Adjust the length of each motion by taking the following steps.

1. Right-click on the first Height Move motion bar. Select Properties from the pop-up menu.

2. Enter a value of *1* (second) for the Length of the motion. Click on OK.

3. Repeat steps 1 and 2 for the second Height Move, with the additional step of changing the Track Start Time to *1* (second).

Finally, edit the position of the key frames by completing the steps below.

1. Right-click on the first Height Move motion bar. Select Properties from the pop-up menu.

2. Select the Path tab. Scroll to the second key frame by clicking on the up arrow at the right of the Current Key value.

3. Click on the Key Setup button and enter a height value of *12*. Click on OK twice.

4. Repeat steps 1 through 3 for the second Height Move, entering a height value of *-12*.

5. Play the animation.

✓ **NOTE:** *When you animate grouped shapes and then ungroup them, you will lose the animation because the "group" no longer exists.*

Animate the second Rod and Piston, using the values in the following table for the roll and height values.

Rod2									
Key frame	1	2	3	4	5	6	7	8	9
Key Start Time	0	.12	.25	.37	.5	.62	.75	.87	1
Roll	0	7	11	7	0	-7	-11	-7	0

piston2_Assy		
Height Move	1	2
Height Value (frame 2)	-12	12

Exporting Animations

As mentioned in Chapter 11, to view an animation outside of Tri-Spectives, you must export it. The level of rendering you choose when exporting will determine the clarity and detail of the animation. TriSpectives uses the active camera view as the basis for creating animation frames. Before exporting, ensure that the camera is looking at the desired point in the scene, and that objects will not move outside the camera's view during the course of the animation. Follow the exercise below to export an animation of the house fly-through.

1. If it is not still active, open the *House_anim.tmd* file created earlier in the chapter. Verify that the animated camera is employed in the current scene.

2. Select File | Export Animation. Choose a folder and file name for the animation, then click on Save. The default animation format is *.avi,* which can be played back using most Windows animation players.

3. Set the Rendering style to Facet shading. For the moment, accept all other default values by clicking on OK.

4. A dialog box will appear, informing you of the number of frames to be exported. This figure is dependent on the number of frames per second (frame rate) and the length of the animation. For a smoother animation, increase the frame rate in the SmartMotion Editor. To limit the total number of frames exported, decrease either the frame rate or the total length of the animation.

5. You will work with the animation in its current state. Click on Begin to initiate the export.

✓ **NOTE:** *To play the animation file outside of TriSpectives, simply locate it in a directory window and double-click on it.*

13

Taking TriSpectives Technical to the Next Level

You now have the information necessary to work effectively with TriSpectives. You have learned to design in three dimensions and to create and edit models and shapes, as well as arrange them in virtual space. You have also learned how to control lighting and texture, employ text and create technical documents, and create animations and export them. This chapter provides a deeper look at possible uses for your newly acquired skills.

There is virtually no limit to the types of models you can create, evidenced by the contents of the standard TriSpectives Technical catalogs. However, there are other sources of information about models, such as the 3D/EYE Web site at *www.3deye.com*. The site contains, among other things, pictures created by TriSpectives users.

Image created by David Millar using TriSpectives.

Image from Web site by Jason Key.

You will also find animations, VRML worlds, and models available for use free of charge. In addition, the site has links to other useful Web pages.

Next, TriGallery clipart libraries are available for purchase from 3D/EYE. They contain well-designed models which will help you reduce the time required to create professional looking 3D worlds.

Forklift model from the TriGallery 4 CD.

Catalogs and Databases

TriSpectives contains translators for importing files, allowing you to use models that have been created in other software packages within TriSpectives. Several 3D model catalogs are available in computer stores. Libraries containing free models are also available on the World Wide Web. In addition, a few service bureaus sell licenses that allow use of their 3D models. Check out the Web addresses listed below for more information.

```
http://www.sdsc.edu/vrml

http://www.viewpoint.com

http://www.3dcafe.com

http://www.acuris.com

http://www.infografica.com

http://www.zygote.com

http://www.ywd.com
```

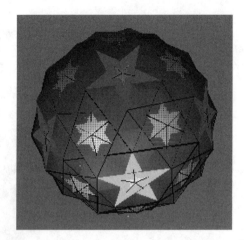

Model downloaded from the Internet and translated into Tri-Spectives Technical.

In addition to 3D models, you may want to start collecting images to use as backgrounds, textures, and gels. There are dozens of CD-ROMs available at computer stores which contain scanned textures and background images. The quality of the scan will directly impact the appearance of your models, so consider carefully before you buy. In addition, you can save images from the World Wide Web with an Internet browser; however, be sure to pay attention to the copyright provisions of images found on the Web.

Creating Custom Catalogs

As you develop worlds using TriSpectives, you may find yourself relying on certain models. Get in the habit of developing your own catalogs. Remember that catalog objects can be modified, allowing you to update your own catalogs when desirable.

You can also create catalogs specific to a particular project or product line. For instance, if you were a manufacturer of skating related products, you could create a catalog for skateboards and another catalog for ice skates. Alternately, you could use catalogs to record a project's design history by saving the design to a catalog at each step in the development process.

Catalogs can be sent to coworkers or clients to be used in TriSpectives Technical or other programs. If you have a local network, you can share catalogs by keeping them in a single centrally located area. However, if you decide to do this, confirm that you have established file permissions. Otherwise, you may end up with models that change unexpectedly.

Virtual Manufacturing

A new and exciting concept still under development is called "virtual manufacturing." In virtual manufacturing, companies could create 3D models of components they manufacture and embed them with useful information, such as material specifications, prices, part numbers, and order desk phone numbers. The models could then be made available to other businesses to be used in design.

For instance, assume an auto manufacturer is designing the car of the future that will require magnetic bearings. The car designer could browse through a catalog of 3D magnetic bearing models and choose the one that best suits the car's design. The other parts of the car would be designed or chosen from existing catalogs, and a complete 3D model of the car would be created. Once the design was approved for manufacturing, a complete bill of materials would be generated from the embedded codes. The parts manufacturer would receive an order for magnetic bearings, and the car would roll (or fly) out in record time.

TriSpectives Technical brings virtual manufacturing one step closer by allowing you to create catalogs of manufactured parts and distribute the catalog to clients. Of course, you may have to apply a trick or two to get your order desk information embedded in the parts.

Virtual part "stamped" with the manufacturer's information.

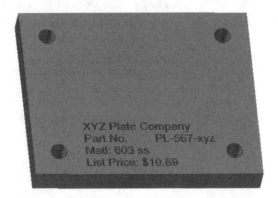

Other Uses

Presentations for the World Wide Web

Global access to the Internet has created new ways of presenting information. You can use TriSpectives Technical to create images, 3D models, and animations which can enhance Web pages. You can even post a catalog file containing TriSpectives objects (models, textures, background images, surface finishes, animations) for other TriSpectives Technical users to download and use. You can also attach a Universal Resource Locator (URL) address to a TriSpectives model prior to exporting it as a VRML model.

Virtual Reality

You can use TriSpectives Technical to create virtual worlds for games, architectural design presentation, and even training videos. Manufacturing videos could be created to show exactly how each piece of a product fits together; the videos would employ exploded views and articulated assemblies. In situations where safety is critical, such as high-radiation working environments, workers could review processes and all tools and parts necessary for a project long before they enter the work site.

TriSpectives Technical can be used to design products, packaging, offices, buildings, cities, or space colonies. The only limit is your imagination.

Index

More OnWord Press Titles

NOTE: All prices are subject to change.

Computing/Business

Lotus Notes for Web Workgroups
$34.95

Mapping with Microsoft Office
$29.95 Includes Disk

*The Tightwad's Guide to Free Email
and Other Cool Internet Stuff*
$19.95

Geographic Information Systems (GIS)

GIS: A Visual Approach
$39.95

The GIS Book, 4E
$39.95

*GIS Online: Information Retrieval, Mapping,
and the Internet*
$49.95

INSIDE MapInfo Professional
$49.95 Includes CD-ROM

Minding Your Business with MapInfo
$49.95 Includes CD-ROM

MapBasic Developer's Guide
$49.95 Includes Disk

*Raster Imagery in Geographic Information
Systems* Includes color inserts
$59.95

INSIDE ArcView GIS, 2E
$44.95 Includes CD-ROM

ArcView GIS Exercise Book, 2E
$49.95 Includes CD-ROM

ArcView GIS/Avenue Developer's Guide, 2E
$49.95 Includes Disk

*ArcView GIS/Avenue Programmer's
Reference, 2E*
$49.95

ArcView GIS /Avenue Scripts: The Disk, 2E
Disk $99.00

ARC/INFO Quick Reference
$24.95

INSIDE ARC/INFO, Revised Edition
$59.95 Includes CD-ROM

*Exploring Spatial Analysis in Geographic
Information Systems*
$49.95

*Processing Digital Images in GIS:
A Tutorial for ArcView and ARC/INFO*
$49.95 Includes CD-ROM

*Cartographic Design Using ArcView GIS and
ARC/INFO: Making Better Maps*
$49.95

*Focus on GIS Component Software,
Featuring ESRI's MapObjects*
$49.95

Softdesk

INSIDE Softdesk Architectural
$49.95 Includes Disk

INSIDE Softdesk Civil
$49.95 Includes Disk

Softdesk Architecture 1 Certified Courseware
$34.95 Includes CD-ROM

Softdesk Civil 1 Certified Courseware
$34.95 Includes CD-ROM

Softdesk Architecture 2 Certified Courseware
$34.95 Includes CD-ROM

Softdesk Civil 2 Certified Courseware
$34.95 Includes CD-ROM

MicroStation

INSIDE MicroStation 95, 4E
$39.95 Includes Disk

MicroStation for AutoCAD Users, 2E
$34.95

MicroStation 95 Exercise Book
$39.95 Includes Disk
Optional Instructor's Guide $14.95

MicroStation Exercise Book 5.X
$34.95 Includes Disk
Optional Instructor's Guide $14.95

MicroStation 95 Quick Reference
$24.95

MicroStation Reference Guide 5.X
$18.95

MicroStation 95 Productivity Book
$49.95

*MicroStation for Civil Engineers
A Design Cookbook*
$49.95 Includes Disk

Adventures in MicroStation 3D
$49.95 Includes CD-ROM

101 MDL Commands (5.X and 95)
Executable Disk $101.00
Source Disks (6) $259.95

Pro/ENGINEER and Pro/JR.

*Automating Design in Pro/ENGINEER
with Pro/PROGRAM*
$59.95 Includes CD-ROM

Pro/ENGINEER Tips and Techniques
$59.95

INSIDE Pro/JR.
$49.95

INSIDE Pro/ENGINEER, 3E
$49.95 Includes Disk

*INSIDE Pro/SURFACE: Moving from Solid
Modeling to Surface Design*
$90.00

Pro/ENGINEER Exercise Book, 2E
$39.95 Includes Disk

Pro/ENGINEER Quick Reference, 2E
$24.95

FEA Made Easy with Pro/MECHANICA
$90.00

Thinking Pro/ENGINEER
$49.95

Pro/ENGINEER in Practice
$49.95 Includes Disk

Other CAD

Fallingwater in 3D Studio
$39.95 Includes Disk

INSIDE TriSpectives Technical
$49.95 Includes CD-ROM

SunSoft Solaris

*Solaris 2.x for Managers
and Administrators, 2E*
$39.95

SunSoft Solaris 2.* User's Guide
$29.95 Includes Disk

SunSoft Solaris 2.* Quick Reference
$18.95

Five Steps to SunSoft Solaris 2.*
$24.95 Includes Disk

SunSoft Solaris 2.* for Windows Users
$24.95

Windows NT

Windows NT for the Technical Professional
$39.95

HP-UX

HP-UX User's Guide
$29.95

Five Steps to HP-UX
$24.95 Includes Disk

OnWord Press Distribution

End Users/User Groups/Corporate Sales

OnWord Press books are available worldwide to end users, user groups, and corporate accounts from local booksellers or from SoftStore Inc. Call toll-free 1-888-SoftStore (1-888-763-8786) or 505-474-5120; fax 505-474-5020; write to SoftStore, Inc., 2530 Camino Entrada, Santa Fe, New Mexico 87505-4835, USA, or e-mail orders@hmp.com. SoftStore, Inc., is a High Mountain Press company.

Wholesale, Including Overseas Distribution

High Mountain Press distributes OnWord Press books internationally. For terms call 1-800-4-ONWORD (1-800-466-9673) or 505-474-5130; fax to 505-474-5030; e-mail to orders@hmp.com; or write to High Mountain Press, 2530 Camino Entrada, Santa Fe, NM 87505-4835, USA.

Comments and Corrections

Your comments can help us make better products. If you find an error, or have a comment or a query for the authors, please write to us at the address below or call us at 1-800-223-6397.

OnWord Press, 2530 Camino Entrada, Santa Fe, NM 87505-4835 USA

On the Internet: http://www.hmp.com

Purchase Your Copy of TriSpectives Technical 2.0 Today!

Now that you have had a chance to experience the power of TriSpectives Technical 2.0, we think you will agree that it is *the* intelligent 3D design program for every technical professional. **So, as a special offer to owners of *INSIDE TriSpectives Technical,* you can purchase the software for a special price**!

TriSpectives Technical 2.0 comes with a **full 60-day money back guarantee**. If for any reason you are not satisfied with the product, you can return it to 3D/EYE within 60 days of purchase and we will refund the price of purchase in full.

As an owner of INSIDE TriSpectives Technical, you can **save $100** off the purchase of TriSpectives Technical 2.0. This offer is good for purchase directly from 3D/EYE or from any one of our authorized dealers. To purchase your copy or to get more information, please call **1-800-946-9533** (700-937-9000). You can also FAX or mail the following order form to 3D/EYE.

TriSpectives Technical 2.0	$999.95
Discount for owners of INSIDE TriSpectives Technical	-$100.00
Shipping & Handling	$ 19.65
Total	$919.60

Payment

Make checks payable to 3D/EYE, Inc.

Credit Card: ( ) Visa ( ) MasterCard ( ) American Express ( ) Discover

Account Number: _____Expiration Date: _____

Name (as it appears on the card): _____

Shipping information (All orders shipped FedEx 2-Day Economy)

Name _____

Address _____

City _____State _____Zip _____

Telephone _____

Fax To: 3D/EYE, Inc. 770-937-0700   *Mail To*: 3D/EYE, Inc.
                                                                     Attention: INSIDE TriSpectives Technical Offer
                                                                     700 Galleria Parkway
                                                                     Atlanta, GA 30339

Visit our web site at *www.eye.com*.